THE

TAIL

LONDON:

HOULSTON AND STONEMAN,

65, PATERNOSTER ROW.

LONDON :

A. SWEETING, PRINTER, BARTLETT'S BUILDINGS, HOLBORN.

ISBN 978-1-332-24101-9
PIBN 10303001

This book is a reproduction of an important historical work. Forgotten Books uses
state-of-the-art technology to digitally reconstruct the work, preserving the original format
whilst repairing imperfections present in the aged copy. In rare cases, an imperfection in
the original, such as a blemish or missing page, may be replicated in our edition. We do,
however, repair the vast majority of imperfections successfully; any imperfections that
remain are intentionally left to preserve the state of such historical works.

1 MONTH OF
FREE
READING

at

www.ForgottenBooks.com

By purchasing this book you are eligible for one month membership to ForgottenBooks.com, giving you unlimited access to our entire collection of over 700,000 titles via our web site and mobile apps.

To claim your free month visit:
www.forgottenbooks.com/free303001

CONTENTS.

THE TAILOR.

CHAP. I.

THE choice of a trade is too important an affair to be made without due consideration, inasmuch as when it has once begun to be acted upon, it can seldom be altered without involving a great loss of either time or money, and probably of both.

And yet it were better to incur this rather than to hazard the well-being and the usefulness of the man, by compelling the youth to continue at an occupation for which he has no aptitude, or which may be unfavourable to his future health and vigour; but it were still better to avoid, if possible, both the mistake and the inconvenience to which it inevitably leads. There is, doubtless, much difficulty in solving the double question, as to the fitness of a youth for the trade he may seem to prefer, and the suitableness of this trade to his constitution and habits. This difficulty is not, however, wholly insurmountable, and may, perhaps, be somewhat obviated by attending to the following hints : In regard to the first part of the question, it may be well to observe the usual bent of the young mind, in regard to its more sober amusements, and it will, probably, be apparent from this, whether or not there is any aptitude for learning this or that business. If, for example, a boy be expert in

constructing miniature buildings, or furniture, ma-
chines, or clothes, or ornamental articles, and that too
without the advantage of suitable tools, it seems right
to conclude that he is likely to succeed well in his
attempts to learn a trade analogous to his amusement.

As to the second part of the question, it will be
proper to notice the general health of the youth, and
to learn from competent judges, how far he is liable to
be affected by the atmosphere he will have to breathe,
the articles he may have to use, or the habits to which
he must conform himself, in order to his fully learning,
and profitably following, the trade to which he is inclined.   At first thought it may seem desirable to
choose a trade which requires but little hard labour,
and which, moreover, has the reputation of bringing
good wages; but every thoughtful and judicious parent
or guardian will readily perceive that these advantages
are dearly bought, if they have to be purchased at the
expense of future health and continued usefulness;
and they probably will be thus dearly purchased, if
care be not previously taken to ascertain how far the
youth is fitted for the trade, and also, how far the
duties and the habits necessarily connected with it,
are likely to be favourable, or otherwise, to the pre-
servation of his mental and bodily health.   An attention to these or similar precautions will, perhaps, be
found more useful in helping to make a judicious
choice than is the common practice of putting a youth
to a trade for a month or two, on trial as it is called,
but which is frequently no trial at all, as he is most
commonly employed during this time in matters which,
if not quite foreign to the trade, have yet but little
direct bearing upon it.   And if he were put to it at
once, yet it would be of but little use in determining
the question, as the novelty of his situation will suffice
to keep him in good humour for the time, even though
he be really unfit for being permanently employed in

that way; while, on the other hand, the time allowed for trial is too short to allow of its being seen whether the trade is likely to be harmless, or hurtful, to his health. There is a necessity for something of the precaution recommended, even though the trade proposed be merely that of a tailor. It is, indeed, commonly supposed that any one, whatever be his constitution or ability, is competent to learn this trade; and, accordingly, if a boy be of weakly constitution, or of slender capacity of mind, he is put to it, in the full confidence that he is, hereby, disposed of in the best manner; but this is a great mistake, and one that is often fraught with much future inconvenience, if not positive misery. For though tailoring does not, indeed, require much hard labour, yet there are few trades in which there is so constant a demand upon the bodily powers, or in which the consequences of following it closely are likely to be more seriously and permanently injurious to the health. Yet if there be not unremitting attention given to the work while at it, it is impossible either to do it well, or to do a sufficient quantity in a given time, and a failure in either of these respects is sure to be disastrous to a workman, and that too in no slight degree; but any one can see, that to force a feeble or unhealthy boy to sit for ten, twelve, or fourteen hours per day, in a close and hot shop, made yet more unwholesome by the frequently dirty habits or diseased state of the workmen, must effectually ruin a feeble constitution, and will evidently go far to shake and impair even the strongest. Unless, therefore, a boy be healthy and strong, let him not be made a tailor, if his future comfort, well-being, and usefulness in society, be thought objects worthy of consideration; let him rather be put to an out-door, active trade, or even be made a servant, or a labourer, so that he may have an opportunity of improving and confirming his health,

and thus pass through life with tolerable comfort to
himself and advantage to others, neither of which
will he be able to do if he be a sickly and feeble
tailor.   If a lad be of weak intellects he is equally
unfit for the trade with him that has a weak or unhealthy body.   Such a one should on no account be
put to it.   He will never learn it well, and, consequently, will be doomed to hopeless and helpless
poverty if he have no other resources; while the probability is, that he will be so unwisely or harshly
treated by his thoughtless fellow-apprentices, and by
ignorant, unfeeling, depraved workmen, as to become
increasingly feeble, if not wholly and permanently
disordered in mind.   This is no dream, nor is the
picture overdrawn.   The writer has seen not a little
of the evils which he here deprecates, and against
which he wishes to give a timely warning, and he has
also felt severely, during many years, the pernicious
effects of a sedentary and debilitating employment
upon an originally feeble constitution.   Nor should a
boy be put to this trade if he have not an aptitude for
it.   If he really have this aptitude, it will be shown by
his having a settled inclination to be a tailor, and,
farther, by his making efforts, though that be but in
the way of amusement, to gain some knowledge of the
trade.   If, on the contrary, a boy manifests no particular predilection for the business, and makes no
effort to prepare himself for going to it, it may be
fairly concluded, that he will never make such progress in it as to be able to prosecute it with advantage, either to himself or others.   It was long since
remarked by a shrewd observer, and a good judge of
both men and things, that ' many a man has run his
head against a pulpit, who would have made an ex-
cellent figure at the plough tail.'   And another has
said to the same effect, that ' many men in the Temple and the other Inns of Court, have wasted both

their time and their property in vain efforts to become lawyers, who would have made clever and useful watermen at the Temple stairs.' In like manner there have been numbers of men, who have consumed their lives miserably to themselves and uselessly to others, as tailors, who might, and probably would, have been both happy and useful had they been brought up as husbandmen or porters. If there be a want of readiness and cleverness about a lad, if he be slow in comprehending, or unable to remember, the instructions given him—if he cannot be made to perceive what is orderly or exact, neat or tasteful, in regard to his work, or if he be impatient of confinement or restraint, or is habitually inattentive or disposed to indolence or inactivity, he is utterly unfit for the trade, and cannot be expected to make himself a competent workman at it. So well is this understood by clever and industrious workmen, that it has long been a sort of proverb among them, that ' a man had better be a bricklayer's labourer than to be either a slothful or a slovenly tailor.' And they are right in this opinion, for there can be no question that the active and efficient labourer is both a happier and a more useful man than is a tailor of this description. The remark so often made—half jestingly, and half in earnest—that a tailor is but the ninth part of a man, probably took its rise from workmen of this character. There is, indeed, a different story current in the shops as to the origin of this saying, but as it is one that flatters the vanity of tailors it is most probably a fiction. It will be seen that these remarks apply chiefly to boys whose friends can afford to give a premium for having them taught, and who, therefore, have the power of either choosing or rejecting a trade as it may seem to be desirable or otherwise. But where the parties are unable to do this, and the boy has no opportunity to learn any other trade than that of a tailor, they ought even then to 'count the cost' before they put him to it. If his father be of the trade, and is either a journeyman or a little master, he will, in all probability, be too poor to apprentice his son to any other business, so that there is only Hobson's choice; the lad must either learn his father's trade or none. Yet, even in this case, which seems to be one of necessity, it will, eventually, be found the wisest plan to ascertain how far the boy's capacity and inclination are favourable to his becoming a good tailor, before he be permanently put to the business. There is, indeed, in this case, a strong motive for almost compelling a lad to work at the trade, in order thereby to add something to the father's scanty income; but this advantage ought to be resolutely given up, if the lad's constitution and turn of mind be evidently such as to disqualify him from becoming a good workman. The father should, indeed, take care to be quite satisfied upon these points before he consents that his son should remain ignorant of a trade, which, with all its inconveniences, yet justifies what was once said by a father, when pressing his son to learn it, viz. that 'a trade is a valuable gift of God, and has a golden foundation.' But so soon as he perceives that the lad is not likely to make a thoroughly good tailor, let him use all his influence and make every possible effort to procure for him some other and more suitable employment. He may make a good servant or labourer, although he would never become a clever tailor, in which case the advantages accruing to him, in regard to both comfort and profit, will, by a considerate father, be thought an ample compensation for the loss he may incur by the change of his son's occupation. In many cases, however, the apparent unfitness of a boy for the trade is caused solely by his thoughtlessness, or his perverseness; and, in this case, there ought to be every prudent effort on the part of the father to correct what is wrong or defective in the son. If these efforts be made prudently and perseveringly, they will probably succeed in prevailing upon the boy to learn his trade well enough to be able to follow it with both satisfaction and profit; at all events he ought not to be given over at once, or without a fair trial, and thus left in ignorance of a trade which, though it be far less profitable than formerly, is still sufficiently remunerative to a clever and steady workman, to warrant all reasonable efforts towards inducing a boy to learn it if he have the opportunity of so doing. He ought not, however, to make the attempt, unless he be determined to learn it thoroughly, and is willing to make the efforts necessary for that purpose, as without these he cannot succeed. Let it not seem strange that so much is said about the importance of being a good workman—it is said advisedly, and it would be well if every one who intends to learn the trade could be brought to believe, that the necessity for learning it thoroughly was never so great as at the present time.

There is a superabundance of workmen every where, and, on this account, a great reduction of wages has to be submitted to by such as are not clever at their work. It is only the men of first-rate abilities who can reckon upon getting any thing like regular employment, or adequate wages for their labour. The inferior hands must, in these days, expect to get little work, and for this little to be very badly paid. There are hundreds, perhaps thousands, of such men in London alone, who are not employed above half their time, and whose wages are miserably low—consequently, they are in a wretchedly poor and destitute condition. Many of them, however, deserve pity rather than censure, for they were never taught to work neatly and cleverly, or else they were wholly

unfit for the trade, but which they are now compelled
to follow, although by following it they may be said
to starve rather than to live. To prevent the increase
of this large and wretched body of men is the object
of this little book. It is believed that the precautions herein recommended will, if duly observed, tend
to lessen the number of inferior workmen, by keeping
incompetent or otherwise unsuitable persons from
being put to the trade. While, by communicating
such information respecting the trade itself as may
enable a beginner to perceive something of its nature
and requirements, it is hoped that the difficulty of
learning it may be somewhat lessened, and the fa-
cilities for learning it well be proportionably in-
creased. The following pages, therefore, will be
directed to both these ends, and as the information
they contain is the result of the writer's experience
and observation during nearly forty years, it is hoped
they may be useful to such as either intend or are
now learning to be tailors.

CHAP. II.

Among savages, or but imperfectly civilized nations,
it is usual for every one to make his own garments,
consequently, the trade of a tailor has no place among
them; inasmuch as a trade consists in the preparing
or making certain articles, which are exchanged for
money or for other goods. But it is not until society
has made considerable progress in civilization that this
is done. It is then found that, by confining the attention and exertions of an individual to one single
and separate occupation, better articles are produced at, upon the whole, a less cost; and it is at
this point, therefore, that trades commence. Of these,

the Carpenter's, the Mason's, the Smith's, and the Wheelwright's, are perhaps among the first that are introduced; the Tailor's, however, is not the last; for men seem to have been employed in making clothes for others in the way of trade, before they were required to act as Bakers, Brewers, or Butchers. The making clothes seems indeed to be an employment better suited to women than to men; and, therefore, Tailors have generally been considered as a somewhat effeminate class; yet it is a fact, that even among uncivilized nations, who usually are not remarkable for effeminacy, the man commonly makes his own garments, if not those also of his wife and children; and it seems to have been so from very ancient times. There are intimations of this practice in the Bible; which informs us, that ' Israel' made ' a coat of many colours' for his son Joseph; and farther, in another place, that ' no man putteth a piece of new cloth upon an old garment,' which operation, although common enough with us, would have been almost impossible in regard to the thin muslin garments there referred to (similar ones to which are yet worn in eastern countries).

That men were once commonly employed in making up dresses or clothes for females, as well as for males, seems to have been the fact, both in England and some other parts of Europe. They were thus employed in Italy, as is intimated by Shakspere, who, in his play of ' The Taming of the Shrew,' introduces the character of a tailor, whom he represents as having brought home a dress which he has made for Katherine, and there encountering, to his real dismay, the pretended violent anger of Petruchio.

As regards England, the practice seems to have formerly been very general, and there are even now some traces of it remaining—as, for example, in the articles of stays, riding-habits, and pelisses, which are still made by men.

As to the antiquity of the trade in this country, it seems to have been well established at a comparatively early age. This appears from the fact of the ' Merchant Tailors of London' having been formed into a chartered company early enough to elect Richard the Second a member of their body ; and farther, from Shakspere's play named after that monarch, in which he gives a humorous account of a blacksmith listening with eager attention to ' a tailor's news.' By the way, the dramatist might as well have told us the errand on which the tailor went to the smith's shop, for, as it is, it seems as though he neglected his work for the sake of an idle gossiping, and thus justified the charge of indolence long since made against his fraternity, and which even now is so frequently repeated. ' Be it known,' therefore, ' to all whom it may concern,' that it was formerly, and probably is now, in some places, the custom of the village tailor to take his iron goose to be heated at the smith's forge. We will, therefore, for the credit of the trade, presume that, in this instance, he had either to take his iron to be heated, or to fetch it home for use, and availed himself of the opportunity hereby afforded for telling the news of the day to his friendly and inquiring neighbour. By this conjecture, (and is it not a plausible one ?) the tailor's character for industry is at once saved, and we see that, although the smith's ' iron on the anvil cooled,' to his manifest detriment, the more prudent and considerate tailor continued to ' drive business,' even while indulging himself with a little recreation. Doubtless, Shakspere knew all this—for what did he not know, relative to men and manners ? He was, therefore, guilty of a wilful suppression of facts, and ought to have been amerced in damages, fixed by a jury of tailors, for thus leaving the fair reputation of a brother snip under so dark a cloud of suspicion.

But, apart from all pleasantry, it ought to be known, for the credit's sake of both a large class of men and of their trade, that tailors are not, as a body, justly chargeable with indolence. Nor have they much temptation to this vice, seeing that they generally work at piece-work, *i. e.* for so much per garment, and in this case their earnings depend upon their diligence ; or, if they work by the day, *i. e.* at so much wages for a given time, they are then tasked, and the man who cannot or does not perform his task of work, or, in the tailor's phrase, ' keep up to his log,' is pretty sure of being speedily dismissed by the master. There is, therefore, in either case, every inducement to diligence, and it may be safely affirmed that these inducements are not ineffective ; for by far the larger number of tailors are as perseveringly industrious men as could be found in any other trade.

This, however, is a digression, yet it seems proper to answer a charge so commonly made and so pertinaciously adhered to ; for were it founded in truth, it would affix a lasting and deserved disgrace upon the whole body of tailors; unless, indeed, it could be shown, that there is something in the trade itself which naturally leads to indolent habits; and in either case it would be a serious fault on the part of parents or guardians to allow a boy to go to the business.

It may have been that this disreputable character was given them on account of circumstances, in regard to which, whatever else they were guilty of, they were certainly blameless. It was formerly the customary practice, in the small towns, the villages, and secluded country parts of Great Britain, Germany, and other countries, for the tailor, with his apprentices and sometimes his workmen, to go to work at the houses of his customers. As there would necessarily be a considerable interval between the times of his going to the same house, there would frequently be a somewhat large accumulation of work, both in making and mending: this would, of course, make it necessary that he should continue there for several days, or perhaps for a week, or even longer. It is not surprising that the coming of the man who was to put all the family into their best trim, should be looked for, by both young and old, with some degree of pleasurable expectation. Such indeed was the fact, and, therefore, when the tailor made his appearance, it was the signal for a scene that was more like a holiday than a serious attention to business. The elder people were glad of a little gossip with one who probably was more conversant than themselves with the news of the day, while the younger ones found ample amusement in the novelty of the scene, and in either playing with or teasing the apprentices or workmen. Meanwhile both these and their master were plied with ample refreshments in the shape of ale, homemade wine, cakes, or the like, between meals, and at meal-times were expected, and almost compelled, to eat as much as would serve for ploughmen or threshers. Thus situated, it was altogether impossible for them to do much work; indeed, work would, in this case, necessarily become a secondary consideration; the first being to contrive to get as much ease as might be possible, under the pressure of too much repletion. The consequence of all this was, that but little work was done. It was indeed day-work, but then there was no tasking. When night came, the wages were considered to be due, and at the proper time were cheerfully paid, whether they had been earned or not; but upon this point there was in fact no need for the tailor to be troubled, since none but himself or his helpers could tell whether or not the workmen were worthy of their hire.

This easy mode of working was, doubtless, acceptable to the tailors, and that it was duly appreciated by them is manifest from their giving it the designation of ' Whipping the Cat;' hereby intimating that they were at these times not much more beneficially employed than if they had really been employed in the flagellation of that useful animal.

From these circumstances, probably, arose the opinion that tailors are habitually indolent. They confessed their fault in this instance, and an uncharitable use was made of that confession; but there is no reason to question their industry at other times. When thus employed, they had a powerful temptation to consult their ease, and they doubtless complied with it; but when they worked at home, and their adequate support depended entirely upon the amount of their earnings, the probability is that they were then, as has been just hinted that tailors are now, quite as diligent as any other class of workmen.

But, be this as it may, the temptations of the ' cat-whipping' days are no longer prevalent. Tailors have long since almost universally ceased working at the houses of their customers; and, therefore, whatever may be the degree in which they indulge themselves in indolence, the consequent loss is their own. And as to over-repletion when at work, they well know, as their own proverb intimates, that ' a half-starved tailor works the best,' and, consequently, there are not many who allow themselves to either eat or drink intemperately except on holidays, or at other leisure times. At the present time, indeed, they have a tolerably good security against habitual excess, in their much reduced and still decreasing wages, which, in most cases, are not more than enough to procure a bare subsistence. Thus much may suffice in vindication of the general industry of tailors. In continuation of this account of the trade, it would be proper to notice the varieties of dress in different countries, together with the changes of fashion among such nations as from time to time vary the shapes of their garments. But this would require a large volume, rather than one or two small pages. The changes of fashion in England alone, during the course of the last few centuries, have been almost innumerable; and they have been as various as numerous. So remarkable, indeed, have our countrymen long been for their versatility of fancy in regard to dress, that there is a pleasant story of a painter, who, being employed to depict the costumes of different nations, when he came to the Englishman, painted him naked, with a roll of cloth under his. arm, alleging as the reason for so doing that he was so fanciful that it was impossible to know what fashion would please him, and therefore he had left him naked, and given him the cloth, in order that he might cut out and make his garments in the shape that, for the present, best suited his fancy. And in allusion to this ever-changing taste, there was formerly at the door of a clothes-shop in the city of London the image of a naked boy, who also bore a roll of cloth, with this significant inscription, ' I would be clothed, if I did but know the fashion.'

But though painters and ready-made clothes-dealers may safely afford to ridicule the frequent changes of fashion, it is not for tailors to do so; as it is upon these variations that they depend for a great portion of their employment.

CHAP. III.

HOWEVER trifling ·a matter it may be in itself, whether clothes be cut and made in either one mode or another, it is not a trifling affair to him who has to gain a living by making these clothes. Tailors, therefore, if they do not, as indeed they cannot, all assist in leading or introducing the fashion, ought, in every instance, and as a matter of positive duty, to adopt any and every new mode of either cutting out or making up garments, as soon as possible; and should moreover take all possible care to learn that mode perfectly.

Nor ought they, as tailors, ever to complain of any fashion that is favourably regarded by the public, however odd or unreasonable they may consider it to be. When, however, it is laid by for one that is newer, and thought to be more becoming, they may then safely criticise it; but while it is in favour, let them keep their private opinion of it to themselves, and endeavour to follow it as closely as possible.

This advice addresses itself to masters, journeymen, and apprentices. To the latter, indeed, it is of great importance, in order to their future success, that they early learn to observe the fashions very carefully—and farther, that they endeavour to put their work together in an exact and neat manner, so as not to spoil the appearance or the fitting of a well-cut garment, which is easily done by a careless and slovenly workman. As apprentices usually begin somewhat early in their apprenticeship to attempt making their own clothes, it may not be amiss to advise them not to be careless in making them because they are for themselves; but rather to take extra pains and care to make them well and fashionably. Nor will they in this case have any difficulty in doing so, inasmuch as, when making their own garments, they are not often straitened for time. Nor should any one, who wishes to succeed well at the trade, shrink from resolutely grappling with what may be troublesome or difficult, as well as strange, in a new fashion. The master will better consult his own interests by explaining and recommending to his customers a new mode of cutting or making up garments, than by waiting until they tell him of it, and express a wish to have their clothes made in accordance with it. The journeyman must not be unwilling to be again a learner; much less must he refuse to be so, contenting himself with repeating the hackneyed shop-board saying, that ' an old dog cannot be taught to learn new dances;' he must rather make every possible effort to adapt himself both speedily and cleverly to the required change. And the apprentice must not imagine that it will be time enough when he becomes a journeyman or a master to be clever in imitating new fashions, but should be willing to believe, what is strictly true, that if he does not while he is young acquire a readiness in learning a new mode, there is but little reason to hope that he will possess it when he is older. All this advice may, indeed, seem needless or trifling to a slothful or careless tailor, but all others will acknowledge that it deserves to be carefully followed.

While on this subject a few words of advice to parents, on the choice of a master, will be neither out of place nor superfluous. An intelligent active boy who likes the trade, will, indeed, learn his business in spite of many and serious disadvantages ; but even he will learn it sooner, and consequently be sooner able to make it profitable to himself, by being placed with a suitable master. The more careless lad, however, will perhaps through the whole of his future life suffer loss from not having been placed with either a com-

petent or a conscientious master ; and there are, un-
happily, too many masters who are deficient in the
one or the other of these respects.

Care should be taken to choose a master who is
deficient in neither, for if he be incompetent to teach
an apprentice he ought not to have one bound to him,
however conscientious a man he may be ; while, on
the other hand, if he be either unprincipled or otherwise vicious, the probability is that proper pains will
not be taken to teach the apprentice, or, if he does
not much neglect him in this respect, that his example will be seriously if not fatally injurious to the
boy's moral principles and character.

Whether a boy be apprenticed to what is called a
little or a large master, may, at first thought, seem to
be a matter of no consequence.   It is, however, of
considerable weight, and deserves to be considered by
all who can afford to choose betwixt the one and the
other.   There are both advantages and disadvantages
in either case : for example, if a lad be apprenticed to
a large master he will be far more likely to have
opportunities of seeing a closer attention paid to the
fashions, and also to see a greater variety of garments
made, than if he were put with a little one.   Moreover, if he be intended in due time to become a master, he will be able to learn the methods of conducting
a large business in a tradesman-like way.   But these
advantages are likely to be quite balanced, if not
overweighed, by the bad consequences that may ensue
from his being obliged, before his principles are fixed
or his character formed, to mix with a large number
of workmen, the majority of whom will be likely, both
by their example and their conversation, to have a
baneful influence upon his morals.   There is also the
farther danger of his attention being called from his
work by the follies and frolics he will have to
witness, and this may beget a habit of carelessness

that will ultimately prove seriously prejudicial to his interests.

The writer has seen much of these evils, and bears witness to their frequency; he has, indeed, seldom seen an apprentice thus circumstanced who has succeeded in becoming either an industrious or a clever tailor during his apprenticeship. Some of these idle and careless youths do indeed make a better use of their time afterwards, but it is evident that even these are considerable losers by their former imprudence, being obliged to spend their own time—and sometimes money also—in order to learn that which they both could and should have learned at the expense of their masters.

There are not, however, many of these young men who are inclined, even if they have the ability, to make these sacrifices; the majority of them, therefore, either continue to be very inefficient workmen, while others become tailors' porters, or ' trotters' as they are technically called, in allusion to their being almost continually ' on the feet,' in waiting upon either the master or his journeymen.

These evils will probably be avoided by apprenticing the lad to a little master, who is also an industrious worthy person and a good workman; but in this case, the greater part of the advantages connected with being put to a large one must be foregone. Yet there is good reason to hope that this disadvantage will be more than compensated by the benefit accruing to the lad from being regularly under the control of an upright and sober man, who knows his trade, and who is conscientiously desirous of seeing his apprentice become a clever workman.

If a lad takes pains to learn all he can or may learn from a master of this description, he will, when he becomes a journeyman, readily adapt his hand to other, and—to him—new modes of working; and also, to the making of such garments as he has hitherto not been accustomed to make, or to see made ; as for example, military and naval uniforms, court dresses, ladies' riding-habits, pelisses, and the like ; or if, when his apprenticeship is expired, he immediately becomes a master, he will, without much difficulty, learn the fashions as they succeed each other, and be able to conduct his business in a way creditable to himself and satisfactory to his customers.

But if, after all, it be determined to put a boy into a large shop, much of the mischief to be apprehended may be avoided by stipulating that he shall, from the first, be put under the care of a sober, industrious, and experienced workman, who shall have authority given him to enforce attention to the work, and while on the board to watch and control his conduct in other respects. It should be the care, as it is the duty, of the lad's parents or guardians, to see for themselves that this agreement is strictly fulfilled ; not allowing themselves to trust implicitly to the representations of the apprentice, who, if he be carelessly or viciously inclined, will, though sure to be a sufferer thereby, think it better to have it broken than kept.

He will not, however, be put at once and entirely to the needle, unless it be previously agreed upon that he shall be, as it is the general rule to employ much of a boy's time during the first two years of his apprenticeship in waiting upon the master or his foreman, keeping the cutting-room and sometimes the workshop in order, going on errands to the draper and the trimming-seller, taking home clothes, and the like ; and no judicious parent will object to his being thus employed during the time above named, as it is indeed necessary to his future usefulness that he should well understand these and similar matters. It should, moreover, be kept in mind, that his health is less likely to be impaired by his being gradually accus-

tomed to work on the board, than if he were wholly
confined to it from the first.

CHAP. IV.

In what has been hitherto said, reference has been
made to all the parties concerned; but in what
follows, the apprentice alone will be addressed, and
he is earnestly advised to follow the ensuing directions, as he will thereby be the sooner able to be useful to his master, and he will probably find that his
personal comfort will be advanced in proportion to his
usefulness.   He is moreover requested to bear in
mind, that although some of these directions refer
more especially to a large trade, yet that he will find
them generally applicable to a small one.

Among his first duties as an apprentice will be the
care of the cutting-room and workshop; these he will
be expected to sweep and otherwise to keep in an
orderly state, and he should be told beforehand, that
in each of these he may either make himself very useful, or do much mischief, accordingly as he is attentive
and careful, or the contrary.   The cutting-room will
require to be thoroughly swept every morning at least,
and perhaps also at noontide.   In order to prevent rais-
ing a cloud of dust, which ought always to be here carefully avoided, he must sprinkle the floor with clean
water; but if, as is sometimes the case, it be covered
by a carpet, he must then use moist tea-leaves, or any
other wetted substance that will allay the dust without
soiling the carpet, or making it too wet. Before, however, he moistens the floor, he must take care to take up
from it every thing which may be useful, and that
may have been accidentally or otherwise placed there.
He will probably find paper patterns, either in whole
or in part, of different garments and for different cus-

tomers ; and these should be put into their proper places. As he will at first, unless previously instructed, be often unable to distinguish between such pieces of paper as are patterns and such as are not, he will find it difficult to decide as to what should be preserved, and what swept away. To assist him, therefore, in this matter, he will find it useful to look at the engraved plates.* The first series of figures represents the different parts of a pair of trowsers. Fig. 1. is the outside thigh of the trowsers; Fig. 2. is the inside thigh; Fig. 3. the waistband. The second series is a waistcoat. Fig. 1. is the waistcoat forepart; Fig. 2. is the waistcoat back; and Fig. 3. the collar. The third series is the patterns of the different parts of a coat; Fig. 1. is the body, or forepart; Fig. 2. is the skirt; Fig. 3. is the back; .Fig. 4. is the outside sleeve; Fig. 5. is the lappel; Fig. 6. the collar. These are usually hung upon nails, or pegs, in the alphabetical order of the names written on them, and the corresponding letters, from A. to Z. placed above them, so that the putting them up properly is no difficult matter, while the contrary is often productive of much trouble and loss of time. He will also be likely to find pieces of cloth which are too large for shreds, and probably skeins of silk or other threads ; also twist, buttons, and it may be pattern books, measuring tapes, with many other articles, each of which should be properly taken care of. He had better by far be a little over-careful in these matters than not careful enough, for it often happens that what may seem to one who is unacquainted with the business of but little or no use, is, nevertheless, of considerable importance ; and much trouble often ensues from the losing or overlaying a paper pattern, or a small piece of cloth, or other material, when it happens to be of any particular colour.

* See page 71 and following pages.

C

The cutting-board must also be put in order; rolls or other large parcels of silk, linen, calico, padding, canvas, &c. must, if they are in a partly unrolled or unfolded state, be neatly rolled or folded up, and put upon the counters, or the shelves, where such articles are usually kept; in short, whatever has been taken out of its place and not put back again, should now be carefully put away. New garments should be put upon the clothes-horse, or wherever else it may be the master's custom to have them placed, and great care should be taken to fold them so that they be not creased, or otherwise be made to look rough and unfinished. They should, moreover, before the room is swept, be covered with wrappers, so as to keep them free from dust, or otherwise soiled.

Such garments as may have been cut out, and have not yet been given to the journeyman, are commonly tied up and laid on the cutting-board till wanted; care should also be taken of these that they be not untied, so as to become intermingled; and if the master or foreman have left a garment on the board only partly cut out, it should be the care of the apprentice, after having removed it for the purpose of cleaning the board, to replace it in the same position as that in which he found it; and, also, to put the measures-book, measuring-tape, rule, or yard-wand, marking-chalk, and shears, or scissors, in such places as that they may be conveniently ready for use whenever they are wanted. It ought to have been remarked, that after the room has been sprinkled it should be allowed to remain for a short time before it is swept, otherwise it will be impossible to sweep it thoroughly, as the dust will adhere to the floor, and cause it to be both smeared and dirty. After the room has been well swept it should also remain a few minutes before the dust is wiped away from the board, shelves, chairs, &c. or they will be covered with the falling dust so as not afterwards to look as though they had been properly cleaned. The workshop will also require daily cleaning, and if it were to be swept and dusted twice in each day, it would be better both for the convenience and the health of the men. The work-board must not, of course, be sprinkled or otherwise wetted before being swept, but it should be well and carefully swept, and wiped clean from dirt and dust. Sleeve-boards, irons, iron-stands, and holders, should be put into convenient places, the irons into the oven or stove, if there be one, so as to be ready for use when wanted. Each journeyman's work should be laid by itself, and the apprentice is bound to see that he does not intermingle one man's work, or trimmings, or tools, with another's. He should also take care not to sweep away any thing among the shreds which is of the same colour and texture with any of the garments in hand, for by so doing he may put both journeyman and master to considerable trouble, and the latter perhaps to some expense, to repair the loss, or, what is yet of more consequence, prevent a garment from being sent home to the customer by the specified time, and thus hazard the loss of that customer. The floor of the workshop and the approaches to it ought to be well sprinkled before being swept; shreds and pieces of every description that are not of any use in the trade should be taken away entirely, and not suffered, as is too often the case, to accumulate in large heaps under the work-board, or in corners, until they become moist or mouldy, and, thereby, tend to make the always unwholesome atmosphere of a tailor's workshop still more baneful to the health of the persons working in it. Let him not think these directions to be either needless or trifling, for he will find his account in attending to them, both in regard to his own health and comfort as well as those of the men's, and he

will farther find that the men will be willing to take
trouble to teach him his business, and to do him service in other ways, in proportion as they see him endeavouring to promote their convenience and comfort.
He should also keep the windows of the shop well
cleaned; this is an important matter, especially in the
very ill-lighted shops so common in London and
other large towns. There is much care and some
judgment required in regard to the proper management of the grate, or the oven, in which the irons
have to be heated. If it be an oven, the apprentice
is bound to see that it is regularly swept, and if need
be wiped with a cloth, so as to remove the dust or
the soot, which usually accumulates there, owing to
there being chinks or cracks in the sides or bottom
of the oven. If this be not attended to, the irons,
instead of being quite clean as they ought to be
when required for use, will be covered with a coat of
black matter that takes up time to remove, which
a journeyman ought not to be obliged to spend in
that way, and which, moreover, when his work is in
a hurry, as it very often is, he does not know how to
afford; and yet, if he does not clean his iron well, he
runs the hazard of soiling and perhaps of quite spoil-
ing his work. The apprentice, therefore, should see
to this matter carefully and regularly, and also to the
keeping up a proper fire in the furnace or grate, as
the case may be: much time is lost and much serious
inconvenience is frequently produced through this
being neglected, and it certainly is the proper duty of
the boy to attend to it wherever there is a boy employed in the business. No good-disposed and industrious lad will wish to throw the care of the fire
upon the workmen, nor will he refuse to clean or to
quench the irons that may be wanted for use. With
regard to fuel, he must take such as the master pro-
vides, and sometimes this is very unsuitable. Many-

masters have a notion that any rubbish will burn in a
furnace; but this is a great mistake, and more especially so if the fire in that furnace be intended to
perform such work as thoroughly heating irons of
from sixteen to twenty or twenty-two pounds' weight.
Yet, it is not necessary that large or even shingly
coals should be used for this purpose. Small coal
and kitchen cinders partially sifted, mixed, and made
moderately wet, will compose a fuel sufficiently strong
to make and maintain a good fire. If the lad cannot
procure a proper supply of these articles, the men
should assist him by making a suitable representation to the master, and such a representation will not
often be in vain.

If the irons are heated in the kitchen grate, and
this is often the case, both the journeymen and the
apprentice will find it to their interest to take all possible care of the fire, and, as far as they can, to heat
their irons at such times as are most convenient to
the mistress of the house or to the female servants.
Many men and lads are highly culpable herein; they
seem to forget, or not to know, that this method of
heating tailors' irons is productive of serious and frequent hinderance in regard to household affairs; they
ought, therefore, to do all they can to lessen this inconvenience, whereas they frequently act as if their
object was to increase it. But hereby they ultimately
injure themselves, for neither mistress nor maid will
do any thing to help them in getting their irons heated.
When, however, a man or an apprentice shows a
concern to avoid giving needless or untimely trouble,
and is, moreover, willing to take a little care of the
fire whenever he has an opportunity of doing so, he
will generally find that pains will be taken to do him
a service in return, and, consequently, he will seldom
fail of getting a hot iron when he wants it. And this
is no trifling matter; on the contrary, it is one of

considerable importance, as, indeed, is intimated by the import of the phrase, so common on the part of the workmen, that ' the iron is the best tailor.'

The apprentice, especially, should guard against showing this carelessness of household convenience, as, if he does not, it may often lead him into much trouble; for as he will, probably, be held responsible for the irons being properly and duly heated, he will, if he does not secure the good-will of his mistress or of the maid-servants, be likely to fail, and that too very frequently, in the performance of this duty, and thus incur the ill-will of the men and the displeasure of his master. He need not be told, if he have only common intelligence, that a lad thus situated is in no enviable condition; his best efforts should, therefore, be directed towards the avoiding bringing himself into it.

It was formerly the custom for the apprentice to make iron-holders * and press-cloths† for the use of the men. It is not so usual now, but if a lad were to provide such articles, and keep them in a clean and perfect state, he would thereby be likely to insure a return of good offices from the men, who usually are very ready to instruct an obliging and attentive boy.

* These should be made of woollen materials, as cotton or linen transmits the heat of the iron to the hand both so soon and so powerfully as to make it very difficult to use them. They should be made so as to bend over the handle of the iron, somewhat after the manner of a saddle on a horse's back, or they will continually be falling off, and thus give much trouble to the workman.

† These are made of two pieces of woollen cloth cut in the shape of a sleeve-board, and sewn together at the sides and at the largest end, near to which end a slit is cut across one of the pieces, and at this opening the board is inserted. The use of the press-cloth is to facilitate the smoothly pressing of thin fabrics, such as linen or cotton; and also to preserve white or other light-coloured articles from being soiled by coming into close contact with the board.

Another duty devolving upon the apprentice, is that of dividing parcels of thread into separate skeins. This requires to be done carefully, or much of it will be wasted by its getting into a tangled state. To prevent this, the whole quantity in one parcel, which is commonly a quarter of a pound, should be drawn over the knees, which should be kept far enough apart to prevent the thread from being at all loose. He will find that the parcel is tied round with a thread of a different colour; this must be cut, and the skeins taken off as smoothly as possible; they are then shortened by folding them into one-fourth of their real length, and tied with a kind of slip knot, so as to be easily undone. The whole should then be put carefully away, so as not to be exposed to the action of the air, as this will soon untwist the thread, and make it so loose and weak as to be unfit for use. The same precaution is necessary in regard to sewing silk, twist,* balls of cotton, and all sewing materials, which are both soon and greatly injured unless closely wrapped up.

He will also sometimes have to match cloth with a pattern, either from his master's stock or at the draper's shop, as also buttons, twist, facings, linings, &c.; and here he will find it necessary to learn well how to distinguish, not only betwixt one colour and another, but also between the various shades of the same colour; or he will often cause himself much needless trouble in correcting mistakes, and probably put his master to both inconvenience and extra expense. He must not allow himself to be persuaded by the draper, or the trimming-seller, to take any article which he does not himself perceive to be of exactly the required colour or shade. And he will

---

* Twist is a thread composed partly of silk and partly of wool, and sometimes, as is the case with mohair twist, of wool only. It is used for making button-holes.

find, that a little attentive observation will soon enable
him to judge for himself as to what is, and what is
not, a good match.

Brushing, or otherwise cleaning,* folding, and pack-
ing clothes, are also among the duties of an apprentice,
and if he learn to be neat and expert in these operations, he will find it to conduce to both his present
comfort and his future benefit.   Much depends upon
these matters, in regard to the appearance of a new
garment.   If they be carelessly slurred over, the best-
made garment will exhibit a slovenly and unsightly
aspect.   In brushing, care must be taken to use the
brush in the proper direction, viz. from the top towards
the bottom of the garment, so as that he may follow
the course of the nap, or, as it is called by tailors, ' the
wool.'   And he must take care, while brushing, never
to move the brush alternately forwards and backwards,
as is the practice in scrubbing a floor, or in cleaning
shoes; as this will make the surface of the cloth
rougher than before it was brushed.

In folding garments, he must see that he does not
put them more out of shape than is absolutely necessary.   If they are to go only a short distance (in
being sent home), they will not need to be folded into

---

* If they be of linen or cotton fabric, and are soiled by the
handling of the workman, they may be tolerably well cleaned
by rubbing them carefully with a piece of clean soft bread.
Starch, finely powdered and pressed through a muslin or other
fine linen bag, by knocking it upon the soiled place, is often
useful. To take out grease spots from woollen garments, spirits
of turpentine may be used with good effect; or if the smell of
this be objectionable, sal-volatile may be substituted for it, and
will be found to answer the required purpose equally well.
Whichever of them is used, the same process is to be observed
in applying it. A piece of woollen cloth is to be wetted with
the spirits, and then rubbed briskly, and also with some exertion
of strength, upon the part requiring to be cleaned; and in the
course of a few minutes it will be freed from the grease.

a very small compass; but if they are to be sent to any considerable distance, and in a packing-case, they must be packed in as close a manner as is at all consistent with their being kept in a tolerably smooth state. The exact manner in which they should be folded is not easy to be described; nor, indeed, is it of much importance that any specific mode of folding should be pointed out, were it more easy to do so than it is, since any lad of fair intelligence and cleverness will readily contrive a method of doing this both neatly and conveniently. He will only want to keep in mind the necessity of keeping the clothes (to be packed) as free as possible from the danger of being tumbled or creased. And he will have ample opportunities of seeing that both these evils may be nearly avoided by a little careful management.

In taking home clothes to the customers, he will often have garments for different persons, and therefore he must take care to place them in his parcel, or over his arm, in such order, as that he may have that garment uppermost which is first wanted. This precaution will prevent tumbling the garments into a rough state, and also the danger of delivering them at the wrong places. If he takes parcels or cases (containing clothes) to the coach, waggon, or packet office, he must on no account either leave them or lose sight of them, if he can prevent it, until he sees that they are properly booked by the person receiving them. If he neglects this precaution, the consequence will probably be that parcels or packages will sometimes be irrecoverably lost.

CHAP. V.

But it is now time to pass from these preliminary duties, in order to give some directions respecting the use of the needle. It must not, however, be thought, because these duties have been dwelt upon prior to saying any thing about the use of the needle, that the apprentice is not at all instructed in sewing until he has made himself master of these. The fact is, that boys are usually put to the needle when not otherwise wanted from the beginning of their apprenticeship. But these other avocations have been classed together, and first named, for the purpose of insuring some degree of orderly arrangement in the contents of this little treatise. And here it will be proper, before giving directions for sewing, first to enumerate the different kinds of stitches, and then to explain, as clearly as may be possible, the manner in which each of them is done. And, first, as to the different sorts of stitches, which are—the basting-stitch, the back and fore-stitch, the back-stitch, the side-stitch, and the fore-stitch; also the back-pricking stitch,* the fore-pricking stitch,* the serging-stitch, the cross-stitch, and the button-hole stitch; besides which there is a distinct kind of stitch for hemming, filling, stotting, rantering, fine-drawing, prick-drawing, over-casting, and also for making what are called covered buttons. The basting-stitch is a long and slight stitch, intended to be merely temporary, or to fasten together

---

* The only difference between these stitches, and the back-stitch and fore-stitch is, that the needle is not, as in them, turned up, and brought back through the cloth, but is first put entirely through, and then passed back again, so as to ensure a thorough hold being taken of the cloth on each side. It is used in thick fabrics, where great strength of workmanship is required.

some of the inner and concealed parts of the garments. It is commonly used to keep the work in its proper position while being sewed.

The back and fore-stitch is made, as the name implies, by the union of back-stitching and fore-stitching; in this stitch the needle is first put through the cloth, and turned up in as short a space as is possible, so as to make a neat and strong stitch when completed; it is then put through the cloth again in the same place as at first, and again turned up, taking care that it passes through the cloth as nearly as possible within the same space as before. This being done, the first back-stitch is completed. The second stitch is made by passing the needle forward upon the surface of the cloth, but without taking hold of it, over a space equal to the length of the first stitch; the needle is then again put through the cloth, turned up, and brought back to the place where it was last put through, so as to form another back-stitch; which is followed by another putting of the needle forward, or, in plainer terms, another fore-stitch, and so on, in the same order, until the seam is finished. This kind of stitch is used for sewing linings, pockets, flannel garments, and other thin fabrics. There is no need to say much respecting the back-stitch, as this may be understood from what is said above respecting the first stitch in back and fore-stitching. This stitch is used for seams where strength is required; it is also sometimes used for ornament, instead of the side-stitch, but in this case it must be very neatly and regularly made.

The side-stitch is used for the edges of garments, to keep them from rolling over, or from being drawn out of shape. It is always intended for ornament as well as use, and requires a very quick eye and a careful hand to do it well. In this stitch the needle is passed through the cloth a little above or below the

place from which it came out in the former stitch, but
it must be at a very little distance from this place, or
the sewing silk will be visible on the surface of the
cloth, which is a great blemish, and yet it must be
far enough away from where it came out to prevent
its breaking through, in which case the stitch is lost,
both as to use and ornament.   Care must also be
taken, that the stitches are at regular distances from
each other, and that the whole of them are placed at
the same distance from the edge of the cloth.   In the
fore-stitch, as has been already hinted, the needle,
when drawn out from the seam, is always put forward, so that an equal quantity of thread, or a stitch
of the same length, is visible on each surface of the
cloth.

Serge-stitching is done by passing the needle
through the cloth, from the under to the upper piece—
throwing the thread over the edges of the cloth so as
to keep them closely together.   It is also used to join
selvages together, as also to prevent taking up more
space for seams than can be spared, when the pieces
are barely large enough for the required purpose.   It
is not, however, much used by tailors, except where
no great degree of strength is required.

The cross-stitch is formed by two parallel rows of
stitches, so placed as that the stitch in the upper row
is opposite to the vacant space in the lower one, the
thread passing from one stitch to the other in diagonal lines, thus—

It is used for keeping open the seams of such garments as require washing, and also for securing the
edges from ravelling out, in such fabrics as are too

loosely made to allow of their edges being fastened down by the filling-stitch.

In the button-hole stitch, the needle is first put through the cloth from the inner to the outer surface, and before it is drawn out the twist is passed round the point of the needle, and kept in that position till the needle be drawn out to the full extent of the twist; this forms a kind of loop, called by tailors the 'purl,' at the top or edge of the opening, and, when regularly made, is both useful and ornamental. To increase the strength of this stitch, and also to aid in making it true or exact, a 'bar' is formed on each side of the opening, before the hole is begun to be worked. This 'bar,' as it is called, is made by passing the needle from one end of the opening to the other (one, two, or more times), so as that there is a layer, if it may so be called, of twist stretching along its whole length (and on each side), upon which the whole is worked, the workman taking care to keep the 'bar' as near to the edge of the opening as is possible, without allowing it to come over, in which case the button-hole will be neither strong nor neat.

There is not much need to say any thing about the hemming-stitch, as almost every lad will have had opportunities of seeing this used by his mother, his sisters, or other females. It may, therefore, suffice for this to say, that care must be taken to set it regularly, and also as closely together as may be either convenient or sightly. It must also be observed, that the needle is not to be deeply inserted, as it is necessary that the stitch should be as little visible as is possible on the other side of the cloth. The hand moreover must not be drawn in roughly, or by a snatch, but so gently as to prevent contracting the hem.

The filling-stitch is similar to that used in hemming;

D

the chief difference being in the direction given to the needle. In hemming, its point is directed outwards, or from the workman, but in filling it is directed inwards, or towards him, and in each should be a little, but only a little slanted, in order to give the sewing a neat appearance. This stitch is used for sewing on facings, and when made with neatness, and without showing itself much on the outer side of the cloth, is considered to be ornamental, as well as useful.

Stotting (pronounced stoating) is the stitch used for joining pieces of cloth so neatly as that the join shall be but little visible, and yet strong enough to prevent the pieces from being easily parted. In this kind of seam the pieces of cloth are not laid the one upon the other, as in back-stitching, but are placed side by side, the edges being carefully fitted, so as to prevent any irregularity or roughness in the work. They are then sewn together by passing the needle half through the thickness of the cloth. Care must be taken to keep the stitches as near to each edge of the cloth as can be done without incurring the danger of its breaking through. The needle is put in on the nearest edge of the two, and must not be slanted in the direction given to it, but put as straight forward as possible. The stitch should be drawn close enough home to prevent the silk thread from showing itself on the right side of the cloth, but yet not so close as to draw the edges into a ridge. If the join be as neatly made as it may be, it will, when properly pressed, be barely perceptible. This stitch is used for joining the pieces of cloth of which facings, collar-linings, and other fillings-up of the inner sides of garments, are made, and also in other cases to prevent the taking up too much of the cloth by making a back-stitched seam.

Rantering, like stotting, is intended to conceal a

join in the cloth. Here, however, it is requisite to make a strong as well as a neat joining; and, therefore, a seam is first sewn with a fore-stitch, and then the rantering-stitch is worked upon or over this seam. It should be worked with a very fine silk thread, or with twist that has had one of the strands taken out. The needle should be both long and slender, and must be passed forwards and backwards over the seam, so as to catch hold of its two sides, and draw them closely together; but, in doing this, care must be taken not to take a deep hold of the cloth: the nap or wool is all that should be taken hold of, and this must be done with a light hand, while the stitches must be placed close to each other, so that the seam may be well covered with wool; when this is done, the seam has to be ' rubbed up,' that is to say, it must be held between the fore-finger and thumb of each hand, these being placed upon the fore-stitching, and its two edges brought as closely together as possible. The rantering must then be slightly carded or scratched, backwards and forwards, with the point of a needle, in order to bring the wool out again where it has been drawn in with the stitch; the seam is then ready for pressing, and, if this operation be properly performed, will be as much concealed as may be necessary; while it will be much stronger than if it had been merely back-stitched.

In fine-drawing, the stitch is formed in the same manner as in rantering, but there is a difference in the way of placing the pieces that are to be joined, *i. e.* if they be separate pieces, for this stitch is mostly used to close up places that have been accidentally cut, or torn; the two edges of the place requiring to be fine-drawn are first trimmed by cutting away the loose threads or ends of the cloth which may be upon them; they are then placed and kept in as level or flat a position as is possible, either with the fingers, or by fastening them to a piece of stiff paper. The needle should be both very small and long, and the thread used, whether it be of silk or twist, should be very slender. Greater care is here necessary than in rantering, to avoid taking a deep hold of the cloth; the needle should be passed forwards and backwards, over the opening, and the thread should be drawn no closer or tighter than is quite needful, in order to hide it in the wool. The stitches must be placed as near to each other as is possible, so as to prevent the edges of the cloth from being visible between them; if it be needful to make a strong as well as a neat joining, the fine-drawing should be repeated on the under side of the cloth, but here it will not be needful to put the stitches so close together. When the fine-drawing is done it must be pressed, but with as light a hand and in as short a time as is practicable, otherwise the sewing, however neatly done, will be visible, and so far as it is so, the design of the fine-drawing stitch will not be answered.

The stitch called prick-drawing is now but seldom used, yet it may be proper to notice it briefly. When this stitch is intended to be employed, the edges of the cloth are first stotted together, after which the needle is passed backwards and forwards in diagonal lines, under the stotting, so as to make the join more strong and durable, than it can be made by merely stotting the pieces together.

This stitch is used where the cloth is very thick, or hard and unyielding, and, consequently, where the stotting-stitch would quickly give way without this support. It is also better than a back-stitched seam for cloths of this description, inasmuch as it can be made to lie more flat, and thus to be more neat in its appearance than a common seam.

Overcasting is used merely to secure the edges of thin and loose fabrics from 'ravelling out.' In using it, the edges of the cloth, whether it be woollen, linen, or cotton, are first trimmed clear of the loose threads; the needle is then passed through the cloth in a forward direction, at about the distance of one-eighth part of an inch from the edge of the cloth, and when drawn out it is carried (from the left to the right, and not, as in other stitches, from the right to the left) about a quarter of an inch; it is then again put through, and on being drawn out it is made to pass over the thread leading from the preceding stitch, so as to form a kind of loop on the edge; which loop secures the edge from becoming too much frayed, or ravelled.

In making cloth buttons, which formerly were almost universally worn, and probably will be again, it is necessary to see that the bone moulds over which the cloth is to be drawn, are all of the same size and thickness. Very thick moulds should be thrown aside, as also should such as are very thin; for the first will make the button too clumsy, and the last will—most likely—soon break. The coverings should then be cut in as near to a circular shape as is easily practicable, and should be cut of that size which will allow of the edges, when turned over the mould, nearly meeting each other. They are then to be slightly sewn round near the edge, and with a running stitch, either a serge or a fore-stitch, according as the material used may require; for if it be likely to ravel much it will be necessary to use the sergeing stitch. When this is done, the edge is gently drawn together, but no farther than will allow room for inserting the mould, which is then put in, as nearly in the middle of the covering as possible. The thread is then drawn tight, so as to bring the edges of the cover close together, and then the needle is passed over the gatherings from the near edge of the button to the opposite one, the maker taking care to keep regularly turning the button round with the forefinger and thumb of the left hand, so as to carry the sewing over every part of the gatherings. The bottom of the button will thus be composed of thread, and therefore may be far more strongly sewn on the garment than if it were fastened on by sewing it merely through the covering.

These brief explanations may suffice to give a general idea of the different kinds of sewing; and this is all that is here designed. It is, indeed, all that can be conveyed in any mere description; and it should be kept in mind that this book is meant to be only such a guide to the learner, as may assist him to learn the more readily when he comes to be employed about what is herein described. This being premised, he will now be addressed as being upon the board, and he will, moreover, be supposed to be placed there for the first time.

CHAP. VI.

THE first thing to be learned here is to sit properly; for until this is mastered, the apprentice will not be able to make much progress with the needle. It were to be wished that some other and better working position could be adopted, but there is little ground to hope that this will be readily done. There have been several attempts made to compass this desirable end, but each has proved unsuccessful. It is indispensably necessary that a tailor should have full command over his work at all times, whether when sewing or pressing, and for all that has at present appeared to the contrary, this can be gained only by sitting in the usual cross-legged position. It therefore behoves the apprentice to make a persevering effort to learn this mode of sitting; and if he will but do this, the inconvenience felt thereby at first will soon be overcome, and then he will be the better able to give his attention to the use of his needle. By sitting in this posture, he will for a time feel some pain across the middle of the thighs, and perhaps in the back also; and this he will do well to bear as long as he can, without being quite distressed by it. When he really needs relief, he may then alter his position in any way that may give it him the most speedily and completely; but he ought not, for his own sake, to allow himself to remain out of his proper working posture longer than is really needful, for in doing so, especially if it be frequently repeated, he will hinder himself from becoming soon enough inured to the position in which he must learn to sit if he intends to be a competent workman. He will, moreover, by letting it be seen that he is willing to make all the efforts he can towards learning this matter, escape the somewhat needless pain to which, otherwise, he may be forcibly subjected. For where lads do not show a willingness to learn, or shrink too soon from a little necessary pain, it is the custom to use a little coercion, and sometimes, indeed, more than a little. In this case, a sleeve-board is placed across the boy's thighs, and kept there by means of an iron goose put upon each of its ends. This is a very painful operation, and one, therefore, which every lad who is careful of his own ease will take pains to avoid undergoing.

In addition to the above-named inconvenience, arising from learning to sit cross-legged, the apprentice will most probably find that his outer ankle-joints will become sore and swelled through being pressed upon the board. This may be prevented by putting a soft pad, or small cushion, under them from the first day of his thus sitting; but if this be neglected, and his ankles are very sore or swell much, he must then take care not to neglect easing them in the way pointed out, or they will probably become inflamed, and may then require surgical assistance. The consequences of all this will be, that he will lose time, which is, at his age, extremely valuable, and his parents will be put to, perhaps, considerable expense in repairing the mischiefs which a little prudential forethought might have altogether prevented.

In conjunction with learning to sit properly, the apprentice will be expected to attempt learning to sew. He will, of course, be provided with needful and suit-able tools; and these are so few and so inexpensive, as to form one of the great advantages which a tailor has over the workmen in many other trades. All the tools that the apprentice or even the journeyman requires, may be bought for a few shillings. A yard of linen for a lap-cloth; two pairs of scissors, one pair moderately large, for common use, and the other small, for button-holes; a thimble; a small piece of bees-wax; and three-pennyworth of needles, are all that he will have occasion to buy so long as he is not a master, or a journeyman working at home, when he must pro-cure a sleeve-board and an iron. The more expensive part of even these few implements, viz. the scissors, will, with tolerable care, last for a number of years with only the trifling expense of being occasionally sharpened by the cutler.

His first job will probably be to sew some linings, or to make covered buttons; and if it be the first, he must take care to keep them clean and without rump-ling, or they will not be fit for use. He must also be careful to sew them with short and regularly-placed stitches; and as the linings will most likely be back and fore-stitched, he must endeavour to avoid drawing the stitch too tight, as this will contract the seam, and also make it likely that the thread will soon break. Care must also be taken to keep the sewing at the proper distance from the edge of the stuff; for if it be too near, the seam will soon ravel out, while if it be too far away, the size of the linings will be reduced, so as, perhaps, to make them too small. While thus employed he should keep in mind that, if he learns to sew linings properly, he will have less difficulty in learning to sew seams of more consequence; and farther, that the more quickly he learns to do plain work well, the sooner will he be put to that which is more complicated, and thus will be the sooner making useful progress in his business.

Should his first job be that of making covered buttons, he will find it useful to have previously committed to memory the directions already given respecting the manner of making them. These directions will assist him to understand more easily what he may be told by the person who may have to teach him when on the board.

When he comes to sew cloth or any other seams, he will soon perceive that the uppermost piece of cloth has a tendency to ' drive,' or ' hold on,' as it is termed by tailors; that is, to slip forward, so as to become much looser than the undermost. This is caused by the manner of holding the cloth when taking the stitch, as any one will readily see who observes that, after the needle is inserted, it is necessary, in order to the bringing it back again, to bend the cloth; in doing which the uppermost piece forms a kind of arch over the undermost, thus making it fuller or wider than the latter; and as this takes place in each successive stitch, it is plain that in the sewing a long seam there will be a considerable length ' driven' or ' held on' in the uppermost piece, thus making it too short for the undermost. But there must be no scissors used here to equalize the length of the pieces, for this would be making what is ' bad' yet ' worse,' as it might wholly spoil the garment. Instead of this desperate remedy the apprentice must use a preventive, and this will be found in taking care to follow these few plain directions.

Before he begins the seam, let him first see that it is basted together both true and smooth, and if it be in a material that is more than usually liable to ' drive,' he will find it useful to baste it with shorter stitches than otherwise there would be any occasion for. When this is done, he must remember to hold the pieces of cloth firmly together between the thumb and forefinger of the left hand; and when he has taken a stitch, it will farther help him, if with the thumb he slightly draw the uppermost piece a little towards the left hand (or from the part already sewed), before he again inserts the needle. In both beginning and finishing the seam, it is well to back-prick a stitch or two, in order to prevent gathering it up into a sort of lump. After the seam is sewn, it has to be ' scratched up,' but if it be in a thick cloth, it must previously be ' bit up.' The first of these operations is necessary, in order to conceal the seam as much as possible; and the second, in order to making it the better yield to the iron in pressing, so as to lie flat or smooth. ' Scratching up' consists in drawing the wool or nap of the cloth over the seam, either with a needle's point, or with the thumb, or finger-nail. This of course is done in a direction opposite to that in which the nap runs, or (as tailors would say) the ' wrong way of the wool.' In ' biting up,' the cloth is opened, or rather drawn out on each side of the seam, until the seam itself can be taken hold of by the teeth; which are then made to bite the two sides of the opening as closely together as is practicable. This done, the seam is ready for pressing, and here great care is requisite, especially if the cloth be of a light or delicate colour, in order to avoid soiling it on the right side, which is in contact with the sleeve-board. It is a good way first to pass the iron a few times along the board; this draws out the moisture which it usually contains, and which is commonly tinged with the colour of the cloth that has previously been pressed thereon. This moisture when drawn out should be well wiped off, and then the seam may be safely pressed, so far as soiling is concerned; but there is also the danger of scorching or burning it, if the iron be too hot. This therefore must, before being used, be tried upon a piece of some light-coloured cloth, and it must not be used on the seam, until it ceases to scorch or discolour the piece on which its heat has been tried.

These directions, however, apply chiefly to woollen cloth, upon which it is necessary that the iron should rest for a short time, in order to prevent the seam from rising. In materials made of cotton or linen, there is no need to let the iron remain; as these are better pressed by being ' knocked down,' or by what may be called ' hammering them open,' with sharp and quickly repeated strokes of the iron.

After the apprentice has learnt to sew seams tolerably well, he will probably be put to the stitching of edges, filling facings, padding lappels and collars, and in due time to the making of button-holes. Each of the stitches used in these, with the exception of that which is used in padding collars and lappels, has been already described, and, therefore, it will here suffice to give a few directions respecting the padding-stitch only. In making this stitch, the lappel or collar must be held in the position in which it is intended to sit when the garment is made. To secure this purpose, it must be held over the ends of the left-hand fingers, in the proper position, while with the thumb the padding must be slightly pushed forwards, so as to make it a little fuller than the cloth to which it is being sewed. The sewing is first carried from one

end of the piece to the other, and is then repeated in
the contrary direction, so as that each stitch in the re-
turning row or tier is made to correspond with that
in the foregoing one, and thus when completed forms
a figure of this sort—

The stitch used, is formed by first inserting the needle
at a point corresponding to the uppermost angle at
the right hand extremity of this figure, marked 1, and
bringing it back again as near as possible to the place
where it was put in. Thus the first stitch is formed :
the needle is then passed forward to the point marked
2; it is there put in and brought out in a direction
corresponding to the second angle in the upper row;
and so on, until the whole row or tier of stitches
is made. Care must be taken to avoid letting the
thread be too much visible on the cloth underneath,
and also to leave a space equal to about a third of an
inch between the sewing and the edges of the lappel
or collar. The apprentice will then for the present
have done his part of the work, and will better learn
what remains to be done by observing how a clever
workman does it, than he possibly could by any either
written or verbal directions. He is therefore requested
to make this observation attentively, as thereby he
will soon be competent to do himself that which he
sees to be both easily and cleverly done by another.

In order however that these preliminary directions
may not extend to an inconvenient length, they will
be here concluded, and in what follows, the apprentice will be supposed to be entrusted for the first time
with the making of an entire garment. Here also he
will derive great aid from attentively observing how
the best workmen proceed in making a garment of
the same kind as that upon which he is employed. It

behoves him, moreover, to ask directions of these men, and for his encouragement he is here apprised that all needful directions are (generally) very cheerfully given to a learner, if he but show a teachable disposition, and also a willingness to do his instructors any little service he may have it in his power to render them.

But, after all, a little previous instruction will be found very useful, and therefore it is here offered him, in the hope that he may avail himself of it. It will be assumed, that his first attempt at entirely making a garment will be made upon a waistcoat, and here, as in other garments, he will do well to follow the course that is pointed out.

CHAP. VII.

WHEN he begins this garment, let him first see that he has got all the necessary pieces for pocket welts, facings, collar, &c. also the proper quantity of lining and sewing trimmings, together with the proper number of buttons, and, if any thing be wanting, it will be the best plan to name it immediately to the master or foreman. By doing this, he will avoid the unpleasantness of being suspected to have lost it, (through carelessness,) as he probably will be, if he defers mentioning what is deficient until he wants it for use. This being done, he will proceed to 'mark and fit up.' By 'marking up,' is meant the marking the proper places for the button-holes, buttons, and pockets; and by 'fitting up,' is meant the cutting the unshaped pieces of cloth intended for collar welts and facings into their proper shapes and sizes.*

* If the waistcoat be of cloth, or any material having a wool or nap upon the surface, he must, as far as possible, contrive to

E

He will learn what these are in respect to the collar.
either from the men around him, or from a paper pattern cut by the master or foreman. When he has done
this, he will do well first to join the several pieces of
which the facings are to be made, as also the collar-
lining, back-seam, and whatever else that may require
joining.   He will thus lessen the number of separate
pieces, and consequently, the danger of losing or of
overlaying them.   The next thing to be done is to
' mark up' the foreparts—the button-hole (*i. e.* the
left) forepart being laid uppermost.   Upon this, he
will probably find two chalk lines, the first running
across, which shows where the pocket-holes are to be
cut ; and the second going down the front, which
marks the distance from the edge at which the buttons are to be put.   If these lines are not quite regular, he must make them so, and then, upon the
buttoning line, he will mark the distances from each
other, at which the button-holes and buttons are to
be placed.   The proper places for the top and bottom
buttons will probably be marked upon the line made
by the master; but if not, his safest plan will be to
ask the direction of a workman.   When he has carefully marked these distances with his chalk, he will
run a thread into them, which by being made to pass
through both the foreparts, will at the same time
mark the places for the button holes and the buttons.
He will take care to leave the thread considerably
loose between the several places at which he inserts
the needle, otherwise he will not have length enough
on each forepart for a sufficient mark.   There must

let all the pieces in the facings be cut so as that the wool will
run in the same direction in all of them ; and if the material be
of a striped or figured pattern, he must take care to match the
stripes, or figures, as exactly as he can, especially in fixing the
pocket welts: which if not correctly sewn on, are a great blemish
upon a waistcoat, however well-made it may be in other respects.

be a thread run, in the same manner, along the line that marks the pocket-holes, and then the foreparts must be separated. In doing this, the marking-threads must first be drawn close in upon the side where they are loose, and this will leave enough thread between the foreparts for the necessary mark upon each. This thread must be cut in the middle, so as to make the marks equal in length, and if each of them be a little twisted with the end of the finger, which should be a little moistened, it may prevent the inconvenience of having them accidentally drawn out.

The pocket welts must now be sewn upon the forepart, and it will be found much better to do this before the pocket-holes are cut than afterwards, as hereby the danger of rending the foreparts is altogether avoided. When the seams are sewn they must be scratched up, and then cut open and pressed. The welts are then to be turned in, so as to be about three quarters of an inch wide, or if a little less it will be none the worse. The pockets are then to be basted in; and then the edge of the welt must be neatly side-stitched; and there must also be a stitching under the seam of the welt, after which one-half of the pocket must be filled near to the edge of the welt, and the other fastened both strongly and neatly to the fore-part. It is then ready to have the ends pricked down, each with two rows of stitches, which must be done carefully, so as to have each end of the pocket-hole inclosed between the rows. It is necessary before pricking the welts, to baste a piece of linen from each end; so as that one may reach the side-seam, and the other the front edge of the fore-part; this will serve to prevent the forepart from soon rending or breaking out at the ends of the pocket-holes, and therefore it is called a ' stay.'

The pockets are now to be sewn round the edges with a back and fore-stitch, and are then ready for

being pressed. The next thing to be done is to baste
in the shoulder-paddings, which must be fastened to
the forepart, at the shoulder seams, round the arm-
holes, and at the end of the pocket welts. At the
bottom and along the front edge it can be fastened
with the same basting-stitch as that which secures the
edges of the foreparts, which are now to be turned in
and side-stitched; after this the button-stay is to be
put on and fastened to the forepart by a small circular
shaped sewing round each place where there is to be
a button, in order to prevent the straining of the buttons upon the forepart from tearing a hole in it.

This done, the collar must be carefully cut the
proper length and a piece marked off, at the hinder
end, just sufficient to go across the top of the back;
after which it must be back-stitched to the neck, and
if it be a rolling-collar, may be held a little tight, for
about three inches from the front end (so as that it
may sit close to the forepart when turned back); from
hence to the shoulder seam it must be a little 'held
on,' and the neck stretched out in the same proportion; or the neck may be stretched first, as much as
is equal to the extra length of the collar, which, of
course, will then require no 'holding on.' This process serves to prevent the neck of the waistcoat from
sitting in a fold or crease, when it comes to be used.
It must be borne in mind, that the collar is on no account to be 'held on' across the back, as this will
cause the back part of the collar to sit badly when
the wearer puts on his coat. It is far better to keep
the collar a little too tight across the back, than to
let it be, though ever so little, 'held on.' Sometimes it happens that the master has cut the collar pattern so long as to require the neck to be un-
usually stretched, in order to put on the whole of
the collar. In this case, the apprentice must not ven-
ture to cut the collar shorter, but must take it with a

forepart and the back to his master, who will tell him what ought to be done.*

When the collar is properly sewn on, the seam must be pressed open, and then the collar-padding must be basted upon the collar, and also, together with the shoulder-padding, be fastened to the seam, so as to keep all both smoothly and firmly together. The collar must then be turned back just so far as to make it of the prescribed width, when, if it fits smoothly and neatly to the forepart, its edge must be turned in upon the padding, with a private running-stitch, and then (all being ready for pressing) it must be slightly pressed along the top, in order to keep it in its proper position. Every thing else that re-quires pressing must be pressed with the same iron as that which is used for the collar, and then the facings are to be carefully basted on. The whole of the edges must then be neatly sewn together with such a stitch as the master may direct, and this will be regulated by the texture, or the substance of the material. If it be a thin and loose fabric, he will probably order the edges of the facings to be turned in, and then to prick the doubled edges together. Here the apprentice should do his best, as much de-pends upon the neatness with which this is done, both as regards the appearance of the waistcoat and the reputation of the maker, and if he will but give his good-will to it, he will soon succeed in pricking edges of this sort so as to make each side equally true and neat. When the edges are finished he may make the button-holes, taking care to cut them all of equal length, with their front ends equally distant from the edge of the waistcoat. It is now the usual practice to cut a small, half-circular-shaped piece out

* The caution here given applies to every other case, where there seems to have been a mistake or oversight on the part of the master.

of the front end of the button-holes, in doing which the button shank, or neck, fits into the hole more smoothly; this, therefore, must not be omitted. After the holes are made they must be ' bit up,' in order to bring their two sides as closely together as is needful, *i. e.* so as that they will just meet; and it is farther useful to fasten them in this position, with a slight stitch, until after they are pressed; but before this is done they should be made as circular at the front ends as is practicable, which is to be effected by putting the pointed end of a bodkin through the hole (until it fills up the open space), and then partially turning it round, while, at the same time, it is gently pulled towards the edge of the garment.

The button-holes being made, it is then proper to put on the buttons, after which the forepart linings must be first smoothly basted, and then neatly sewn in with a filling-stitch; then the back must be put in with a strong back-stitch, care being taken not to let it drop lower than the forepart at the bottom of the side-seam, nor to allow it to rise higher than the forepart at the top of the shoulder-seam, as in either of these cases the back will be shortened, and this may cause the waistcoat to misfit in the neck. The seams being sewn, the back lining has to be filled down upon the forepart lining, just so far over as to cover the sewing of the seams. The strings or straps by which the waistcoat is to be drawn in to the required size are then to be put on, and the waistcoat is ready for being pressed off. This should be done with great care, lest the waistcoat should be scorched, or otherwise discoloured, and particular attention should be paid to the linings, that they be not in any way soiled, nor suffered to go out of hand in a rough or tumbled state. To prevent soiling them, it will be found a good plan to press with a piece of thin and clean stuff, either silk, shalloon, or calico, under the iron, as, after all possible care has been taken to clean this, it will usually soil a light or delicately coloured article unless this precáution be observed.

After the waistcoat is thoroughly pressed, it will be much improved in appearance by giving it a little careful brushing before it be given in to the master. Every workman who wishes to set off his work to the best advantage will cheerfully do this, although it be not required by any rule of the trade. If, however, the material be such as cannot safely be passed under a brush, it will then suffice to whisk it with a piece of clean cloth, whether it be woollen or cotton will not signify, so that it be quite clean. This being done, he may consider the waistcoat to be finished, and may take it into the cutting room to be examined.

Here a caution suggests itself, which it will be well for the apprentice to remember : if the master finds fault with any part of his workmanship, let him be careful not to resent it either by his demeanour or by unbecoming language ; he may think himself justified in showing resentment, because the master is as he supposes more nice than is needful, but be that as it may, the apprentice will best consult his own interests by endeavouring, to the utmost of his power, to meet his master's wishes. Hereby, he will give satisfaction to one whom he is bound to obey, and at the same time will be contracting a habit of carefulness which will be not a little useful to him when he becomes a journeyman.

The foregoing directions have reference to a single-breasted waistcoat with a plain rolling collar, for a plan of which the reader may look at the annexed engraving, p. 75. But the greater part of them will apply also to the double-breasted waistcoat. The chief difference between these two waistcoats lies in the front, or breast, and therefore it will suffice merely to notice the way in which the front of the double-

breasted waistcoat should be made up. The chief
things to be attended to are the holes and buttons,
which require to be very carefully marked, in order
that they may exactly correspond, and thus fit nicely
together when the waistcoat is buttoned. It is also
necessary that the lappels be sewn on without being
at all ' driven' or ' held on,' otherwise the fronts of
the foreparts will not be equal in length, however
exactly the holes and buttons may have been marked.
In sewing the lappel seams the hand should be drawn
tightly in when sewing over the breast, where there
is commonly a little swelling out of the edge, which
requires to be drawn in with the stitch, so as that the
seam may not sit loose or flabby, when the waistcoat
comes to be worn. These directions will equally
apply to the lappels of a coat, and, therefore, the
apprentice should try to keep them in mind with a
view to his future as well as to his present advantage.

Thus much must suffice for instructions in regard
to making waistcoats. The next garments to be considered are the trowsers and the breeches. As regards the trowsers, the first thing to be done is, as in
the waistcoat, to see that all the necessary pieces and
trimmings are given in with them, and if any thing
be wanting, that the master be immediately apprised
thereof, so as to prevent any dispute that might otherwise ensue. The outside thighs should then be fitted
to each other, to see that they are exactly alike in size
and shape, as it frequently happens that there is a
considerable difference between them, through their
having been cut out in a hurry. The inside thighs
should then be examined in the same manner; and
when this is done, the next thing is the basting up the
thighs, preparatory to the seams being back-stitched.
This basting is 'a matter of considerable importance
in regard to the fitting of the trowsers, and, therefore,
should be done with all necessary care; the thighs

should be basted up so as to be both alike in all respects, and as there is frequently a loose or stretched-
out edge at the side-seam of the outside thigh, in consequence of its running parallel with the selvage of
the cloth, and being also near to it, it is necessary to
take care that the fulness caused hereby should be
regularly 'held in' down the whole length of the
side-seam, in order to prevent the thigh from being
twisted, as this will hinder the trowsers from fitting
nicely, however well the master may have cut them.

The seams are now to be back-stitched, and their
width must be regulated by the nature of the material
of which the trowsers are made. If it be any thing
that will not easily 'ravel out,' the seams must be
very narrow, but if it be likely to ravel they must
be wider, and must, moreover, be 'over-cast,' or
'serged,' so as to prevent the ravelling as much as
possible. After the seams are sewn, they must, if
there be a nap on the cloth, be 'scratched up,' and
then they are ready for the pressing, but before
getting the iron, it will be proper to join all the pieces
that may require to be joined, as one well-heated iron
will press the whole, and thus both time and needless
trouble will be spared.

All the seams should now be well pressed, i. e. if
the iron be hot enough for that purpose, but if not,
then the tops and bottoms of all the seams, together
with the pieces, must be now attended to, and the remainder be left until the iron is again wanted. The
facings are now to be basted on, the bottoms of the
trowsers basted up, and, with every thing else that
needs it, got ready for what is called 'a plain sew.'
There is nothing very difficult in either putting on the
facings, or making up the bottoms; the only thing of
importance to be kept in mind is, that both the thighs
of the trowsers are to be made up in exactly the same
manner; that they will require neat workmanship,

both in the facings and the bottoms, hardly needs to be here noticed. In fixing on the strap-buttons great care should be taken to put them on so as to correspond to the holes in the straps, or if the straps be sewn on, then care is necessary in order to their being put exactly in the place prescribed by the master. The tackings of the pocket, or other slits, should be very strong, and at the same time neat, both of which may be easily effected with only ordinary attention. When the tops are made up so as to be ready for the waistbands, there follows a job of some difficulty to a learner, viz. ' pitching the waistbands.' Upon this being done properly a good deal depends as regards fitting, and, therefore, it will be well first to define the term, and then to direct how the thing defined is to be done.

By ' pitching the waistbands' is meant the so placing them upon the tops of the outside thighs, as that when they are sewn on, and the fall-down brought over them, the fall-down seam may run exactly over the middle of the buttons on the right hand waistband front, and in a line with the front ends of the button-holes at the front end of the left hand waistband. At the same time it must be seen to, that the edge at the side of the fall-down just meets the side-seam. If, when the fronts and sides are thus adjusted, the fall-down will lie smoothly from side to side, the waistband is ' pitched' properly, but not otherwise, for, if the fall-down in order to lie smooth must fall short of the side-seam, the waistband is ' pitched' too much forward, while, on the contrary, if it projects over the side-seam, the waistband is ' pitched' too much backward. Both these errors should be carefully guarded against, but especially the latter, which produces very unpleasant consequences to the wearer, who, in this case, will feel himself to be uncomfortably confined across the belly, and, if he be at all corpulent, will

suffer both pain and inconvenience. The first-named
error is not of so much consequence, yet it ought to
be carefully avoided. The waistbands being properly
sewn on, together with the fob-welt and brace-stays,
the whole may then be pressed; after this the pockets
are to be put in, taking care to keep them clean, and
to sew them strongly, and this being done, the thighs
may be joined together, or ' closed' as the tailors call
it, when the top buttons must be put on very firmly,
and also exactly in their proper places, or the ' tops'
will not button ' true and smooth.' The linings are
then sewn, if there be linings, and, with every thing
else that may need it, are pressed. When these are
smoothly sewn in, and it is very important that they
should be, a little farther pressing, in order to all
being thin and neat, will finish the trowsers, which,
as in the case of the waistcoat, will amply repay all
the trouble of a little brushing and trimming up before
they are inspected by the master.

With regard to the making of breeches, there is no
need to say any thing, except as respects the knees;
but these are by far the most difficult part of this garment, and therefore call for much careful and clever
workmanship. If the breeches be intended for
' dress,' as it is called, they will be cut rather short,
just so as to come over the knee-cap, and then the
knee-garter should be kept ' tight' in sewing it
upon the outside thigh; nor will it need to be much
' held on' in sewing it upon the inside thigh, or
' over the ham,' as it is usually called; but if they
be ' riding' breeches, they will be cut rather long,
so as to just meet the swelling out of the calf of the
leg, or, perhaps, so as to come a little lower even than
this; and here the garter must be kept a little easy
across the outside thigh, while the inside thigh, or
' the ham,' will require to be a good deal stretched
out, so as to allow of the garter being considerably

'held on,' otherwise the breeches will not sit well upon the calf, but will be perpetually 'riding up,' or, forcing themselves upwards into the hollow between the calf and the knee-bone. In this case they will be too short, or rather will seem to have been cut too short, when all the mischief has been occasioned by the oversight of the maker in not sufficiently stretching out the ham. In order to make the breeches button close in the hollow part of the knee, *i.e.* between the knee-cap and the rise of the calf, it is usual to put the buttons more in, or farther from the edge, at this part, than either at the top or the bottom of the buttoning, so that the buttons, when on, stand in a curved line. The exact direction of this curve will be determined by the number of inches which the master will name as the proper size of the bottom part and the middle of the buttoning. The top part will be regulated by the knee-slit tacking, with which the buttoning must here correspond. The knee-holes should be both very neatly and very strongly worked, as they are much exposed to the eye, and also are in all cases likely to have much hard wearing. If the garter be intended to have a buckle, it will be needful to make the width of the strap exactly according to the size of the buckle, and to strengthen it by putting a strong stay between the outside and the lining. In 'pressing off' the knees, the 'ham' must be well stretched out, so that the garter may not seem to be at all 'held on,' otherwise the good effect of the fulness which has really been put in, will be in a great degree prevented. There is nothing more of much consequence that needs to be added to these directions, except that both the trowsers and the breeches require to be thoroughly pressed over the entire surface of both the outside and inside thighs, in order to take out the creases which have been made either by the folding of the cloth at the drapers', or in the course of making up the garment. This pressing is farther needful in order to 'take off the gloss' from such parts as have not yet been brought under the iron, and thus to prevent the spotted or clouded appearance that would present itself were one part to remain without pressing while the other has been pressed.

It is proper to observe that the trowsers and breeches here spoken of are supposed to be made with what is called a 'whole fall-down,' but they are sometimes made with a 'narrow fall-down,' which formerly was the general fashion, and will probably be so again ere long. This fall-down requires more nicety in the making up than the other; the bearers and side-welts must be kept rather tight when sewn on to the edges of the fall-down slit; the seams should be small and very regular in regard to their width, and the bottoms of the side-welts must be 'tacked down,' so as to be both strong and neat. They are commonly made of a triangular form, and are called 'pointed tackings;' sometimes they are semi-circular, and then they are called 'round tackings;' and they are at other times made straight, and are then known as 'square tackings.' It only remains to say, that the waistbands are pitched in the same manner as in the whole fall-down, and farther, that if there be any 'fulness' in that part of the inside thigh which is sewn to the hinder part of the waistband, it must not be brought very close either to the side-seam or to the seat-seam, but must be principally 'held-in' over the middle part.

Thus much must suffice for these garments, as it is now time to say something concerning the manner of making a coat; and here, as in the former cases, the first thing to be seen to is, whether or not all the needful pieces of cloth, and also all the trimmings, are given in; if they be not, let them be immediately spoken about. This being done, the coat

F

must be 'fitted' and 'marked up,' but these operations need not be dwelt upon, as what has already been said of fitting and marking up of the waistcoat will, in a great measure, apply to the coat. One or two words of caution may not, however, be needless. It is necessary that all important pieces, such as the outside-collar, the cuffs, the lappels and lappel-facings, and the flaps, if there be any ordered to be put on, should be provided for before the less important pieces are cut. Any other plan of cutting up the pieces given in for facings, &c. will be pretty sure to involve the workman in considerable difficulty, and he may, at the least, prepare himself to be taunted as a cutter, whose only talent is that of being able to cut large pieces into small ones. He may, however, incur a heavier penalty than this, in the displeasure of his master, and probably, also, in his own inconvenience, if not injury; and it will be wise to avoid all these consequences of cutting hap-hazard, by following the advice given above, to which may be added, that he will find it helpful to mark out all the pieces before he begins to cut.

In marking the buttons and button-holes, the same care is required as in the waistcoat, to see that they are made to correspond with each other exactly. The pieces intended for facings, collar-lining, &c. should also be marked with the chalk where they are to be joined, so as that they may be readily and smoothly put together. When all is 'fitted' and 'marked up,' the coat may be made in the following order; not that it is necessary to make it in this, rather than in any other order, but it is well to have a regular method of putting its various parts together, and the method that is now to be pointed out may be found as useful or convenient as most of the others that might be named.

In order to lessen the number of separate pieces as

soon as possible, it is a good plan to begin with stotting the joins of the facings, cuffs, collar-lining, and
whatever else that may require being joined; this is
called 'piecing,' or 'piecing out. When they are
'pieced,' they may for the present be laid aside, and
the backs may be made. These have to be 'turned
in,' and filled and stitched, except there be a cord
or braid to be put upon the edge, and then the stitching is omitted. If the backs have been cut out of the
open or selvage side of the cloth, they will usually be
more or less loose on the edge, or 'fagged out,' as it
is commonly called, and this will make it necessary
to draw in the hand closely, or to put the trimming
on a little tight, so as to make the edges of the backs
as nearly straight as can be compassed. After this,
the flaps, if there be any to be put on, may be stitched,
and the foreparts be separated by cutting the marking stitches in the way already spoken of in treating
of the waistcoat. The flaps are then basted carefully
on, and the ends of them must be neatly pricked
down for about one-third of their length, from the top
downwards. The waist must then be 'closed,' taking care first to stretch out the waist-seam of the
body in the hollow part, in order that the coat, when
on, may sit close to the waist; if there be any 'fulness' in the waist-seam of the skirt, it must be 'held
in' as nearly as possible over that part where the hips
of the wearer may be expected to come. After the
waist is 'closed,' the lappels must be back-stitched
on, taking care to keep the hand tight in sewing over
the breast, for the purpose of preventing the seam
from being loose, or 'fagged out.' This done, the
waist and lappel seams must be carefully pressed;
the fulness, if any, of the skirt-waist being 'shrank
in,' unless the forepart waist requires to be farther
stretched, in order to make it of the required size.
When the seams are pressed, the hip-stays must be

put on, and the side-seams may be ' closed,' taking
care that they be put together very smoothly and correctly: the plaits may then be basted up, and the
pockets put in as smoothly as possible, or they will be
likely to contract the skirt and put it out of its proper
shape.   The pocket-slits should be strongly ' tacked,'
or they will soon break out; the top edge of the
pocket must be securely fastened to the waist-seam,
and if the front of the pocket be afterwards fastened
to the bottom of the lappel canvas, by a stay running
from the one to the other, it will be so much the
better.

After this, the lappel canvas may be put in; it
should first be carefully basted to the forepart, and
then it must be fastened at the seams, and also by a
stitching round each of the button-marks, which will
prevent the button from soon breaking the cloth, as it
is very likely to do, unless it be thus guarded against.
The lappels must now be ' padded,' that is, the canvas must be sewn to the cloth in the manner pointed
out when the padding-stitch was described.   This
being done, the edge of the canvas must be cut away,
so as to fall short of the edge of the lappel about one-
third of an inch.   The stay-tape must now be put on,
keeping it but a little tight along the edge of the
skirt, and plain at the bottom of the lappel; as also
upon the front edge of the lappel, as far as to the place
where it begins to turn back.   From hence to the top
it must be kept tight enough to draw the edge in, so
as that when the lappel is turned back it may sit
smoothly and handsomely, the edge just touching the
forepart; across the top of the lappel, the stay-tape
may be put on nearly level, and it must then be
turned up and fastened strongly to the canvas, by
which means the coat will be guarded against soon
' breaking out,' or rending at the top of the lappel-
seam.

The facings being first got quite ready, by drawing in the fronts of the lappel-facings, to make them correspond to the lappels, all will now be ready for the 'iron,' and must be well pressed,—particular care being taken with the lappels, in order to press them so that they may fall back freely, and to the proper width. The iron should also be passed along the edge of the lappel, where it has been drawn in, in order to press out the little gatherings made thereby, otherwise the edge will be rough and irregular after it is stitched, which is a great blemish. This being done, the buttons may be put on, and then the shoulder-padding may be fastened in, being slightly sewn to the shoulder canvas in order to keep all smooth. This is also the time to put in such wadding as the body of the coat may require, to make it sit smoothly when worn. After all is thus prepared, the facings must be first carefully basted on, and then the back parts must be 'filled,' and the front edges 'stitched' with more than ordinary care, as it is especially needful that the workmanship here should be very neat. The shoulder-facings may then be stitched to the padding, and the body-facings neatly fastened to the wadding, in order to keep the latter from falling down into a lump, which otherwise it probably will do, and thus be useless, if nothing worse.

The button-holes must now be made, taking care that they be worked very true and neat, and farther, that they all be of exactly the same length, and at the same distance from the edges of the lappels. After this the shoulder-seams may be sewn, and if the forepart be longer than the back at this part, the 'fulness' must not be 'held on,' but the seam must be sewn plain or smooth, and whatever there is to spare of the forepart must be carried into the scye, or arm-hole, but on no account into the neck.

The foreparts will now be ready for the sleeves, and

F 2

these, if not already made, must now be got ready.
They must be sewn with a back-stitched seam, and
care must be taken to put them smoothly together.
The cuffs should be carefully made up, in order that
they may be both alike; and a neat button-hole will
here be very desirable. When the sleeve-hands are
tacked over, the seams 'scratched up,' and the linings
sewn, the whole must be thoroughly pressed and well
smoothed all over. The linings must then be put in,
taking care that their seams match exactly to the
seams of the sleeves, and also that the hand-facings
are not put on so as to be at all full, either in width
or length, when the sleeve is turned out. The buttons
at the cuffs are now to be put on, the elbows of the
sleeves tacked to those of the linings, and the sleeves
'hollowed' or 'cleared out' at the top of the inside
sleeve; but this must be done according to the directions given by the master, for it often happens that
sleeves, especially when cut by different masters,
require some difference in the manner of hollowing,
and a mistake here is likely to do considerable mischief. The arm-holes of the coat must now be prepared for the sleeves, by cutting away the paddings,
so as to be about level with the arm-hole, but the
facings should be allowed to project a little over the
edge of the arm-hole, in order that there may be
enough room to sew the sleeve-lining to it without the
risk of its soon breaking out. When this is done, the
sleeves must be back-stitched in, taking care to keep
them a little tight from the side-seam to about the
middle of the underneath half of the arm-hole. From
hence to about an inch over this half the sleeve may
be 'held on' a little, and the arm-hole stretched out
to it in the pressing, which will serve to make the sleeve
sit more comfortably at the front of the arm-hole. The
fulness of the outside sleeve must then be gathered in
with as much regularity as is possible, or it will neither

'press out' nor allow the sleeve to sit handsomely upon the shoulder. The seams being 'scratched up' are now to be pressed, and it is necessary that this should be done with great care, in order to guard against stretching out the arm-hole at improper places, as for example over the shoulder, or near the side-seam, which will be likely. to make the coat misfit. Before beginning to press it is needful to turn the sleeve out a little way, so that the arm-hole may be readily got at while pressing; and it is by far the best plan to press but a short length of the seam at once, as this prevents the danger of either stretching the arm-hole, or of making creases underneath or about it.

After the arm-holes are pressed, the facings must be slightly yet exactly fastened to the seams, and some wadding must be put at the top of the outside sleeve-lining, in order to keep the fulness of the sleeve from sitting badly; after which the linings must be neatly filled round, but with a slack hand, or the stitches will be likely soon to break; and the fulness of the lining must be gathered in so as just to correspond with the fulness of the sleeve; all which being done, and the back-seam also sewn, the coat will be ready for the collar.

As, however, this part of the coat is almost perpetually being altered in shape, size, &c., and as, moreover, it varies so much in different kinds of coats, it is difficult to give such directions respecting it as will meet more than a very few cases, and even these only for a short time. It must therefore suffice for this merely to say, that it should be made as exactly as possible according to the pattern supplied by the master; but as regards sewing it upon the coat it is needful to observe, that it must not be 'held on' in front, or along that part which turns back with the lappel, as this will make the collar sit loose or flabby, and thus spoil the good appearance of the coat of its most conspicuous parts. Neither must it be 'held on' across the top of the back, as this will make the coat sit off (or away) from the neck, and thus make it likely that the top of the collar will be often coming into contact with the hat of the wearer.

To whatever extent the collar may be too long for the neck, and it is always needful that it should be something longer, the fulness must be 'held on' in the space between the shoulder-seams and the place at which the collar turns over; taking care first to stretch out the neck, both the outside and the facing, before sewing on the collar, and also to repeat this stretching both when the seam is pressed open, and when the coat is being 'pressed off.' When the seam is pressed open, the shoulder - paddings must also be again stretched out, so that they may not contract or confine the neck of the coat, and then they are to be serged to the edge of the collar-padding; after which the facings must be smoothly basted over it, and the out-side collar 'filled down' over the whole; particular care being needful that this be done with great neat-ness, as it is in so conspicuous a place. The coat will now be ready for 'pressing off,' and will, however well-made in all other respects, be much improved in appear-ance by this being done thoroughly and cleverly. Much nice and skilful handling is now needful in order to make the fronts of the lappels and the whole of the collar sit handsomely; but the way in which this is to be done cannot be learned by any written directions. It must be seen to be understood. After the coat is pressed, the edges, unless they have been 'turned in,' or have had a cord sewn upon them, must be 'pared off,' that is, they must be very evenly cut away to within a little less than the eighth part of an inch from the stitching; taking care, while paring, to keep them steady, by laying them across a sleeve-board, and also to let the right hand rest upon the thigh so as to pre-vent its shaking, otherwise there is much danger of making an irregular or jagged edge, which is always a great blemish. It should also be observed, that in this operation the blades of the scissors should not be held perpendicularly, but must be a little slanted, so that the uppermost blade may have its edge 'bearing out' or 'inclining' towards the left hand. This will cause the uppermost layer of cloth to project a little over the undermost, and prevent the unsightly appearance that would be caused by the latter projecting out beyond the edge of the former.

After all is duly pressed and neatly pared, the only thing that remains is, as in the other garments, to wipe off any gloss that may have been made by the iron, and to give the coat a slight brushing and trimming, when it will be finished, and may be taken into the cutting-room.

Directions have now been given for making an entire plain suit, which, together with those given for the breeches and the double-breasted waistcoat, will be found amply sufficient to answer all useful purposes. There is, therefore, no need to treat of any other kinds of coats, waistcoats, or trowsers, as each is but a variety of some one or other of such as have already been described. Nor would it be of much use to attempt to describe the way of making fancy garments, such as riding-habits, pelisses, and children's dresses, since the fashions for these are so frequently being changed, that any written directions, however accurate at the time, would soon cease to be of much service. As to the methods of making military and naval uniforms, court-dresses, and the like, these also may be far better understood by seeing them than they can be by any other mode or kind of instruction, while with regard to the first-named of these dresses it ought to be noted, that they are liable to very frequent and great alteration, both as to shape and trimming.

CHAP. VIII.

ALL, therefore, that now remains to be noticed in the way of directions to a learner, is the method of cutting out garments according to the rules followed in drawing the plans in the annexed engravings. And here also, as in the directions for making up, it must suffice to notice a few of the plainest and most usual garments.

The first shall be the trowsers, as in these there is not much that is difficult. It may be well to observe here, once for all, that it is highly important to learn how to measure correctly, as without this the best possible rules for cutting will avail but little when they come to be practically applied. The following measures for plain trowsers will be found sufficient:— 1. From the waistband seam to the knee-bone, and from thence to the bottom, on the outside of the thigh, for the length of the side-seam.* 2. From the fork or crutch to the bottom, on the inside of the thigh, for the length of the leg-seam. 3. Round the thigh, as high as to correspond with the dotted line marked a in the engraved trowsers plan. 4. Then again round the thigh at the part corresponding to the dotted line marked b. 5. Then round the knee, as is represented by the line marked c. 6. Then round the bottom, as shown in the line marked d. 7. And then round the waistband. These measurements are sufficient for all common purposes; while such others as may be requisite for any particular shape or fashion will readily suggest themselves to an intelligent person when he needs them; but it is evident that they cannot be previously suggested to him by another person.

The measure being correctly taken, the next step is to lay the cloth for the trowsers quite smooth upon the cutting-board, taking care that the wool or nap runs

* The figures are shortened in the patterns given.

TROWSERS.

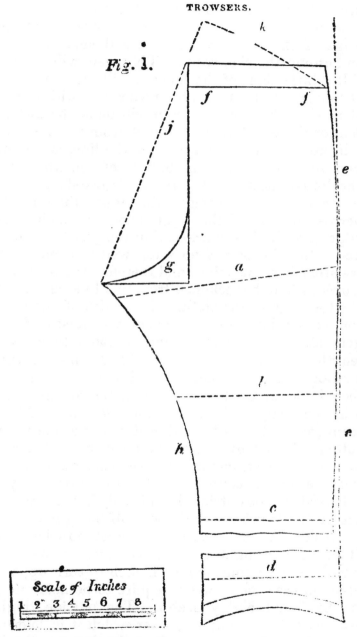

Fig. 1.

Scale of Inches
1 2 3 4 5 6 7 8

The above and all the following Figur
are drawn to this scale.

from the right-hand end of the cloth to the left, or
from the top to the bottom of the trowsers. A chalk
line may then be drawn quite straight along the
edge of the cloth, which line will serve as a guide
in forming the side-seam. This seam will, at the top,
fall a little short of the line ; it will then run out until
it touches it at the hip, from whence it will go in until
it reaches the knee, where it will be at the distance of
half or three quarters of an inch from the line, when it
will go out till it again touches the line, and then will
run upon it down to the bottom of the trowsers (see
the dotted line marked *ee* in the engraved trowsers plan
in page 71). A straight line must then be drawn
across the top of the thigh about an inch from the
edge (see the line marked *f* in the plan). The piece
above this line serves for a top-welt to come upon the
waistband in buttoning, and therefore the length of the
trowsers is to be reckoned from this line, and not from
the top-edge of the cloth. The width of the thigh at
top is regulated by the size of the waistband, being
generally made about an inch broader than half the
length of one waistband. The fall-down seam runs in
a straight line for about two-thirds of its length, and
then in a curved line (drawn in the manner marked
g in the plan) to the top of the leg-seam. The leg-
seam (marked *h*) is formed by drawing a line from the
bottom of the trowsers to the point marked *i*, and at
such a distance from the side-seam as is required by the
measure, the measure being of course divided by two,
or halved, as the outside thigh is only half the intended
size of the trowsers, the other half being made up by
the inside thigh. The bottom must now be marked
either in a straight or a curved line, as may be required, and leaving about an inch to turn up, which
piece, in case the trowsers require to be made longer,
will be found highly useful. The outside thigh is
now ready for cutting out, after which it is laid upon
the cloth, its bottom being brought down to the left-

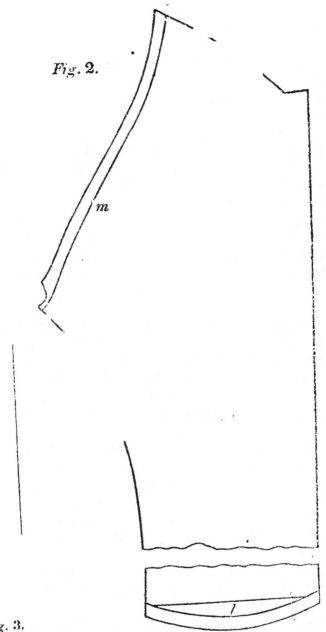

Fig. 2.

m

Fig. 3.

hand extremity thereof, leaving just enough to allow
of cutting a little roundness upon the bottom of the
inside thigh (as seen in the plan, fig. 2, letter *l*), the
leg-seam of which is then marked in a parallel line
with that of the outside thigh, except near the top,
where it springs out a little in order to give more
room to the wearer in striding or in sitting down; after
which the seat-seam is formed by first drawing a
straight line from the top of the leg-seam to a point
on another line, which line is drawn from the hip
cross-wise, by using the top of the leg-seam as a
pivot, and carrying the measure from the hip as far
over towards the seat-seam as is required by the size
of the waistband, which in the plan represents sixteen
inches, eight and a half of which being required for the
width of the outside thigh, there will be seven and
a half left for the width of the inside thigh (seen on
fig. 1, the dotted lines marked *j* and *k*). The seat-
seam (marked *m* in fig. 2) is then formed of the proper
shape, being ' drawn in' a little from the straight line
over the waist, and carried out so as to touch it over
the breech (as is represented in fig. 2, letter *m*). The
space from the inner to the outer line represents a
' laying in;' *i. e.* a piece left on in case the seat should
require to be made larger. The inside thigh is now
marked, and may be cut out, taking care to leave a
piece down the side for a ' laying in;' and, moreover,
either to mark or to cut the waistband of the exact
length. The trowsers are now cut out, and may be
laid aside for the purpose of cutting a waistcoat with
a rolling collar, which garment is now to be considered.

For a waistcoat, the only measurements required are,
the length, and the size round both the breast and the
waist.

Here, the stuff being folded along the middle, so as
that the two foreparts may be cut at the same time, a

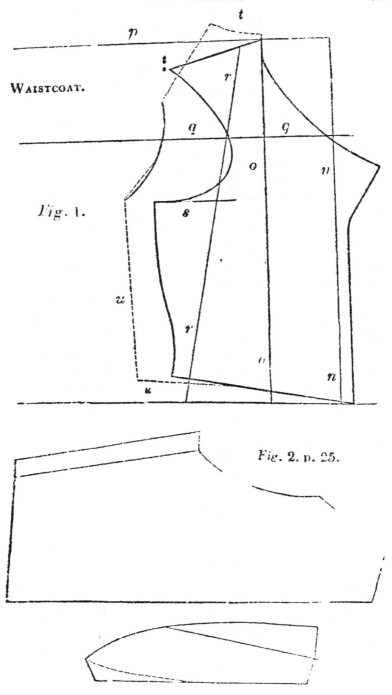

WAISTCOAT.

Fig. 1.

Fig. 2. p. 25.

Fig. 3, p. 25.

line is to be drawn from top to bottom at about the
distance of an inch from the edge; then another line
parallel to this at the distance of a ninth part of the
whole breast measure, which in the preceding engraving represents thirty-six inches, and consequently
the distance between the two parallel lines in fig. 1.
marked *n* and *o* represents four inches. The next
thing to be done is to mark the length of the forepart,
allowing one-sixth of half the breast measure for the
width of the back; thus, if the whole length of the
waistcoat is required to be twenty-five inches, the
forepart, when the one-sixth (*i. e.* three inches) is
deducted, must be twenty-two inches long, exclusive of
the shoulder-seam and the ' turning in' at the bottom.
When this is ascertained, and the two parallel lines
are drawn, the next thing to be done is to carry the
measure from the bottom of the front line, which must
terminate at the bottom edge of the stuff, over to the
farther line, causing it to touch that line at about
twenty-two and a half inches from the bottom, the
extra half inch being for the seam and the ' turning
in.' ˙ At this point a mark must be made, through
which a line must be drawn horizontally, as is represented by the line marked *p* in Fig. 1. After this
another horizontal line must be drawn at the distance
of one-third of the half of the breast measure, or six
inches from the uppermost one, in order to mark the
front of the neck (see Fig. 1. *q*).

Then, at the distance of one-eighteenth of the half
breast measure, or one inch from the top of the second
perpendicular line, a mark must be made, and also
another mark at the distance of four and a half inches,
or one-fourth of the half breast measure, from the bottom
of the same line. When this is done, a line must be
drawn from the one of these marks to the other, as is
represented in the plan by the line marked *r*. By the
help of this the front of the arm-hole and the width of
the forepart at the bottom are regulated—the arm-

hole front, as may be seen, coming about half an inch over the line forwards, and the bottom of the forepart an inch over it in the opposite direction. The next thing to be done is to make a mark upon this line at the distance of one-fourth of the whole breast measure from the uppermost horizontal line; this will be nine inches: and from this mark another line must be drawn horizontally; then, at one-sixth of the half breast measure (or three inches) distant from this mark, another mark must be made, and this gives the top or the side-seam, and also the proper width of the forepart (see the line marked *s*). The side-seam may now be marked, either a little curved, as in the plan, or quite straight. The shoulder-seam is drawn by first making a mark at the distance of one-ninth of the half breast measure (or two inches) from the front perpendicular line, near to the bottom of it; and another mark across this at the distance of one-half of the whole breast measure (or eighteen inches) from the uppermost horizontal line. This double mark forms a pivot for the purpose of striking the line for the shoulder-seam, the end of the measure being fixed on the mark with the left hand, while with the right hand it is carried over from the points where the second perpendicular line forms an angle with the uppermost horizontal one, to the distance of one-ninth of the whole breast measure (or four inches) from the top of the oblique line marked *r r*; and this marks the seam both as to its length and its direction.

The neck-seam is formed by a curved line drawn from the top of the front perpendicular line to the point where this forms an angle with the undermost horizontal line, carrying the curved line as far beyond or over the perpendicular line, as may be required by the fashion or by the height to which the waistcoat is meant to be buttoned up. In the plan it is carried over to an extent representing two and a half inches, which will in general be far enough.

G 2

There needs no directions as to either slanting the bottom of the foreparts, or placing the marks for the pockets, as these matters depend solely upon the prevailing fashion, or upon the fancy of the master; so that when a line is drawn where the buttons are to be placed, the foreparts are ready for being ' cut out.'

This being done, the back must be marked out in the following way. The foreparts must be laid upon the stuff intended for the back, so as that the back-seam shall be parallel with the second perpendicular line, and it must be made to project above the uppermost horizontal line about one-third of an inch. The shoulder-seam of the back will be three inches distant from the back-seam at top, and six inches distant from it at the bottom; or one-sixth and one-third of the half breast measure. The length of the back shoulder-seam is regulated by that of the forepart-seam. The top of the back shoulder-seam will project above the horizontal line about an inch, or rather more: see the dotted lines marked *t t*, which mark the top and the shoulder-seam of the back. The next thing is to mark the side-seam of the back, by first deducting from the half breast measure the width of the forepart, and then carrying the measure out from the line that marks the back-seam to the extent required to make up the proper size. In the plan the width of the forepart represents ten inches near the top of the side-seam, and nine and a half inches at the curve; consequently the half back must be eight inches wide near the top of the side-seam to make up eighteen inches, the size here represented, and as wide at the bottom as is requisite to make up the half size of the waist, which in this case is reckoned at seventeen inches; the half back is, therefore, seven and a half inches wide at the bottom (the dotted line marked *u* shows the side-seam and the bottom of the back). The back arm-hole is formed by a curved line reaching, as seen in the plan, from the lower point of the shoulder-seam to the top of the side-seam. This completes the marking out of the back, which may now be cut out, taking care to leave a piece on at the side-seam in case the waistcoat should require to be made larger.

No better directions can be given for the collar, than that it must in all cases be regulated as nearly as possible by the prevailing fashion, or by the taste of the customers.

It is exceedingly difficult to teach the art of cutting out, either by plans or by written descriptions; nevertheless, a few words must be said respecting the coat, but it should be clearly understood that this will, after all, convey only a vague notion of the manner in which this garment is cut. They may, however, be useful to the learner when he seriously applies himself to the study of the art of 'cutting out.' There are many clever men who teach this, and it is usual for them to have what are called 'cutting clubs,' where, by the payment of a small sum, a young man may not only see the process of 'cutting out,' but also may exercise himself in a practical way. To such a source of instruction as this the learner is earnestly advised to betake himself, if he wishes to learn the art thoroughly, for here he will have all the necessary helps, and at a moderate expense.

For a coat the following dimensions must be taken: 1. The length of the waist. 2. The length of the coat. 3. The distance from the middle of the back to the elbow, and from thence to the bottom of the sleeve. 4. The size of the arm at the top, just above the elbow, at the wrist, and at the bottom. 5. The length of the front, measuring from the top of the back-seam to the bottom of the lappel. 6. The size of the breast just under the arms; and, 7. The size of the waist—to which may be added, the height of the collar.

Here, as in the other garments, the cloth must first be laid smoothly upon the cutting-board, with the wool or nap running towards the left hand. Then a line is drawn along the edge of the cloth (at about one and a half inches distant from it), and the backs of the coat are then marked out. But instead of attempting a long written description, such as those given for the waistcoat and trowsers, it may be as well, perhaps better, to refer the reader at once and altogether to the engraved plan. In this the whole size of the breast is assumed to be thirty-six inches, and all the parts or proportions to be pointed out will have reference to this as a standard. It is hardly necessary to say, that whenever the size of the breast is either more or less than this, all the parts that are regulated by the breast measure will have to be altered in the same proportion.

Fig. 1 is the back, of which the top is three inches wide. From the back-seam to the dotted line at the back scye is six inches. From the top of the back-seam to the horizontal line is also six inches, and if this line were continued so as to touch a continuation of that which marks the back-scye, the latter would be two inches in length. These numbers, respectively, represent one-sixth, one-third, and one-ninth of the half breast measure (viz. eighteen inches). The space between the dotted and the outer line, represents a piece which is left on above the standard width, in order to meet the prevailing taste for wide backs. The length of the waist, and the width of the back at the hip, are altogether governed by fashion. Fig. 2 is the forepart skirt, which is, of course, made of the same length as the back-skirt; the waist (letter *a a*) is generally cut a little longer than the required size, in order to give room over the hips ;* the shape of the front, and the width of the bottom, are regulated by no fixed rule, but vary with the fashions.

* The back part of the waist-seam at the hip drops from the square 4½ inches, or one-fourth of the half breast measure. See Fig. 2. Letters *b b.*

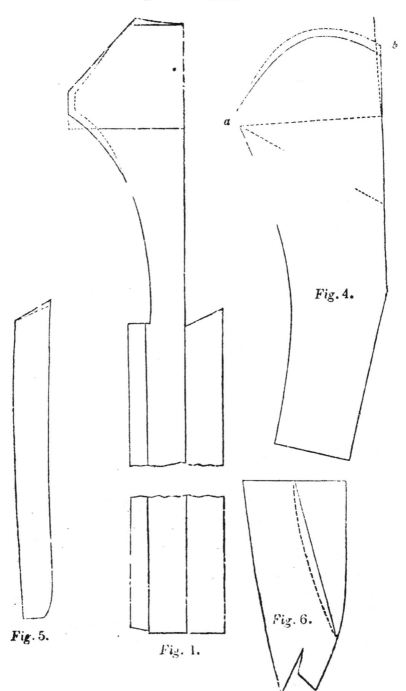

Fig. 4.

Fig. 5.

Fig. 1.

Fig. 6.

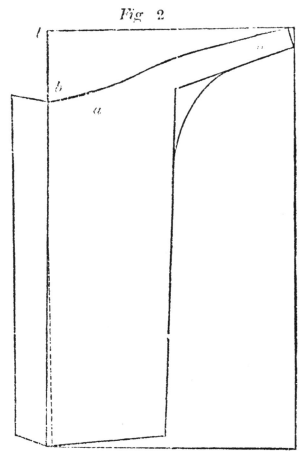

Fig 2

Fig. 3 is the body (with the back annexed to it), and
this is the most important part, as it is also the
most difficult to ' cut out.'   A square is first formed
equal in size to the half breast measure, and a horizontal line is drawn across this square at six inches
from the top.   This line is divided into three equal
parts, each of which, in the plan, represents six inches;
these, with such variations as may be required by the
fashion, will give the width of the back across the
shoulder; the width of the arm-hole from the side-
seam to the front, and the width of the breast, exclusive of the piece which is left on in front beyond the

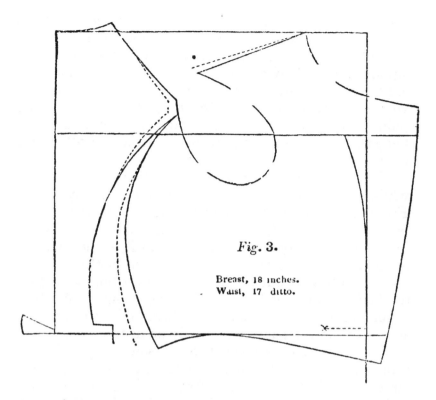

Fig. 3.

Breast, 18 inches.
Waist, 17 ditto.

line of the square, and which piece is wider or narrower according to the width required for the turning back of the lappel at the top, and the size required for he waist at the bottom. The space left in the plan represents three inches (or one-sixth of the half breas' measure). The size of the arm-hole is governed by the size of the breast, and will commonly be found to be an inch, or thereabouts, less in circumference than the half breast measure.

The shoulder-seam is formed in exactly the same manner as in the waistcoat, which has been already described, but would come higher up at the lower point (as marked in the plan), only that a piece has been marked off equal to the extra piece that is marked upon the back. The piece marked off is represented by a dotted line running alongside of the seam, and touching it at the top.   It is necessary to observe, that (in the plan) the upper point of the shoulder-seam is brought forward upon the top of the square about half an inch more than the rule pre-scribes (which gives four inches or one-ninth of the whole breast measure as the proper distance of this point from the front of the square); this is done to keep the coat from dropping in the front, as otherwise it would be likely to do.

The side-seam is governed by that of the back, while that is regulated by the fashion, or by fancy. From about four inches from the top it is ' cut in' from the true line (represented in the plan by a dotted line), by gradually leaving this line until, at the waist, it is about an inch distant from it.   The bottom of the body is hollowed out in the same proportion, and then the body is stretched out to the proper size.   All this is done to prevent the coat from sitting full or in creases across the lower part of the body or in the waist.

The neck-seam is formed in the same way as in the waistcoat, and in like manner varies both in length and direction with the changes of fashion. The length of the body is, of course, governed by the length of the back.

The sleeve, represented by Fig. 4, is principally regulated by fashion, i. e. as to its shape, size, and length; the only thing here requiring notice is, the manner of forming the top of the outside sleeve.   The straight dotted line running across the plan is at the distance of nine inches, or one-half of the half-breast measure from the back-seam.   A piece having been allowed on the back across the shoulders, as has before been noticed, a corresponding piece has to be taken off from the top of the sleeve, which piece is there represented by a dotted curved line.   The width of the sleeve at the place marked by the straight line is eight and a quarter inches, but it would have been nine inches if the arm-hole had not been made smaller than the rule prescribes, i e. eighteen inches, by the addition of the piece upon the back. The point of the fore-arm seam, marked a upon the plan, is fixed by letting it drop from the straight line for about the space of an inch, or it may be formed by measuring nine inches downwards from the top of the hind-arm, marked b, which will reach to the point marked c, and then carrying the measure across the sleeve in an oblique direction upwards, until it touches the fore-arm-seam at the 9th inch, above which place the seam may be carried for about half an inch, as may be seen in the plan. This rule is generally useful, but, like all others, will have to be varied with circumstances, and these varieties must be learned by experience, and made as the occasions may require. The collar is altogether governed by the fashion or by the fancy of either the master or the customer.

It was intended to say something concerning the method of cutting breeches and double-breasted waist-coats, but it is necessary to omit this, as the directions already given have extended to an inconvenient length; and there is, indeed, no such necessity for saying any thing relative to these garments, as the greater part of their more important points has been already noticed. What has been written is the result of much careful practice, and may, therefore, prove useful to a beginner, although the writer could have wished it had been possible to convey his instructions in a plainer, and, to himself, a more satisfactory manner. This, however, owing partly to the nature of the subject, and, perhaps, partly also to his own want of skill in writing, he has found it impossible to compass. Yet, if what he has written be carefully read, always connecting this reading with a reference to the engraved plans, he feels confident that the directions given will be found useful to a mere beginner, and it is for such only that he has ventured to give them.

It may here be proper just to say, that the apprentice cannot too soon begin to turn his attention to this branch of his trade, especially as he will not be likely to receive any instructions therein from his master, for, unless a special agreement be made to that effect, it is not customary to teach the apprentice any thing of the art of cutting out. The indenture speaks, indeed, of his master undertaking to teach him the whole 'art and mystery' of tailoring, and if there be any 'mystery' connected therewith, it must be in the cutting, as it is sufficiently plain that there can be none in the sewing; yet it would seem that the law does not compel a master to teach his apprentice aught about cutting. The writer, in common with many other persons, thought otherwise, until a case occurred under his own eye which led him to form a different opinion. In this case the apprentice, on his master's refusal to teach him, brought the matter before the Lord Mayor of London, when the master succeeded in his resistance, by showing that cutting was a separate and distinct art—that it could be practised by such as knew nothing about sewing—and farther, that many men earned their living solely by practising it.

CHAP. IX.

Thus far the writer's object has been to assist the apprentice in learning to be a clever tailor, and he ventures to hope that the directions he has given will, if followed, be found conducive to this end. But he would fain be useful in regard to a higher purpose than this; for although it be a great advantage to be a competent workman, yet this alone will be of but little real or permanent use, unless it be accompanied by bodily health, together with respectability of character; and, therefore, in what follows, the writer will endeavour to give such advice as may assist in securing or attaining these very important advantages.

By the time the apprentice becomes a journeyman he will, probably, have discovered, that his trade is more or less prejudicial to his health; but as it will then be too late to alter what has been done, his best plan will be to use every possible precaution in order to prevent his suffering more than is quite unavoidable. If he has any due regard to his true welfare, he will not hesitate to sacrifice a little present gratification for the sake of securing a large measure of future benefit. For he may rest assured, that although the life of a working mechanic may be supportable, it cannot be either comfortable or very useful, unless he enjoy, at least, moderately good health. It is, therefore, plainly, of great moment, that all possible care should be taken to secure what is so indispensable to his well-being.

The apprentice has in general but little to do in regard to the providing himself with either food or lodging; and, therefore, must be content to do the best he can with what is provided for him; but even here much that would be hurtful to him may be avoided, and much also may be done that will be directly beneficial. He may not, indeed, be able to regulate the quality of his diet, but he can, and he ought to, regulate the quantity, for it is here that most young persons make a great mistake, and act with great and continual imprudence. No tailor, especially if he have any tendency to disorder of the stomach, can safely indulge in either taking full meals, or in eating, as is often done, a variety of indigestible articles between his meals. If, therefore, the apprentice does either of these things, he will not fail to pay the penalty due to his folly, but will soon find that his stomach is disordered, and he will farther discover what, perhaps, he did not before suspect, that this organ cannot long be out of order without producing other and yet more serious mischief, which, if not repaired, will in all probability imbitter the whole of his future life. In order to avoid so great an evil, let him be careful to both eat and drink tem-

perately, or if need be to restrict himself to a fixed
and small quantity, at the same time taking care to
eat nothing between his meals, and he will soon be
able to know whether or not there is need for these
precautions, by observing the sensations he feels in
his stomach after having taken food.   If he be disposed to costiveness, he will find it useful to take
occasionally a little white mustard seed in the morning as soon as he rises, and he may also find it
·well to chew a small piece of rhubarb an hour before
dinner, but let him on no account indulge in any
excess of either eating or drinking and then take
medicine, as many thoughtless people do, with a view to
lessen or remove the mischief, for, unless in extreme
cases, this procedure does but increase it.   The best
remedy in this case is fasting until the stomach is re-
lieved by the ordinary operations of nature; this may,
indeed, seem to be a somewhat tedious process, but it
is, nevertheless, both safe and inexpensive, and on these
accounts, besides others, is worthy of a patient trial.

It is, moreover, very injurious to make a practice of
taking aperient or any other medicines regularly, or
without considerable periods of intermission, for in
this case the constitution is likely to be both seriously
and permanently injured by the large quantities of
drugs which it will eventually be necessary to take in
order to procure even a moderate effect.   The best
method of restoring the tone of a weakened stomach
is by constantly rising early, taking regular exercise,
which a young and single man can well afford to do,
and observing strict temperance in eating and drinking, taking care wholly to reject whatever he finds
to be unsuitable to his stomach, and this he will
easily ascertain by his own observations, and that, too,
far more exactly than can be learned of any medical
man, however skilful he may be.   Personal cleanli-
ness is also a very important means of preserving the
health, and will, moreover, be found useful in the way

of helping to restore it when interrupted by any ordinary cause. A hint upon this subject is not mis-
placed or needless, inasmuch as tailors are much in
danger of contracting dirty and slovenly habits, and,
therefore, the apprentice cannot too early endeavour
to avoid them, since when once formed they are not
easily broken off. But the chief danger to the health
arises at the time when the apprentice first becomes a
journeyman; until then he has in general the benefit
of being both taken care of and properly advised by
those around him; but as he will now wish to be
quite at his own disposal, it is most likely that he will
forego the advantage of living with his relatives or
friends for the sake of being at full liberty to do
as he pleases. If he have been apprenticed in a small
country place, he will most probably decide upon
leaving his home for London, or some other large
town, where he may see the world, as it is called,
and he will be the more ready to do this on account
of the larger wages he may thereby be enabled to
earn. He is not, perhaps, to be blamed for making
this change, but he ought to be apprised that there is
connected with it considerable hazard both as to his
health, and to his moral character. As regards his
health it is almost certain that it will soon be placed
in jeopardy by a variety of circumstances, some of
which he will not, perhaps, have the power to alter.
Among these may be reckoned damp or ill-aired beds
or linen; unsuitable food; the necessity for often
taking his meals while at work on the board; expo-
sure to great and sudden changes of temperature, both
from heat to cold and from cold to heat; to all of
which must be added, the very probable want of a
comfortable lodging, viz. one where he might be a
little carefully tended or nursed, if need required.
As he will assuredly meet with some if not all of
these perils to his health, and as any one of them is
sufficiently powerful to inflict upon it considerable

injury, it ought to be his earnest concern to learn
how the evil may be the best counteracted, since it
cannot be altogether avoided. As to the first danger,
he may in a great measure avoid it by sleeping between the blankets, until he is assured that there
is no farther danger, which there will not be after the
first few nights ; with respect to his linen, if he have
not access to a fire, he may contrive to make it fit for
wearing by keeping it for a night or two between the
uppermost blanket and the coverlet of his bed.   But
let him on no account put it on just as it comes from
the washerwoman, for he may be well assured that it
will then be too damp to be worn with safety.   As to
his food, he will, so far as dinner is concerned, be able
to get what is tolerably suitable at an eating-house
unless when his work is wanted in a hurry, so that he
has not time to leave the board.   In this case, let him
beware of taking the substitute for dinner, which is
commonly sent from the ' beer-house.'   This usually
consists of ,a newly baked loaf, a slice of single
Gloucester new cheese, and a pint of porter—the
thoroughly indigestible nature of which when put
upon a tailor's stomach is well understood even by
tailors, who, consequently, jocosely denominate them
' sponge, soap, and heavy wet.'   When there is not
time to go to dinner, it will be found far better either
to procure a dry hard biscuit, or even to fast altogether,
rather .than to take these things upon a stomach that
is already weakened by six hours' confinement in an
unhealthy posture, and which at the same time is not
much the better for the breakfast that was taken.
And this leads to a word or two respecting this meal
also : it is usually taken while working upon the
board, as there is no breakfast time allowed to tailors,
whether they work by the ' day' or the ' piece.'   The
articles usually furnished are quite new bread, a slice
of butter, which is not often very good, and a pint of
a strange mixture that is called tea, which, however,

very little resembles the tea made by a good house-wife. Such a breakfast as this cannot fail of being hurtful to the stomach, if it be regularly taken for any great length of time. But it is not now necessary to take it at all, as a good and wholesome breakfast may be procured, and for less money than the bad one, at a coffee-shop, if it be a respectable one—otherwise the difference will not be great. Many men take their breakfasts at such a shop before they go to work, and the only objection against doing so is, that there is then so long a time to wait before they go to dinner : this, however, is no great evil, perhaps none at all, but if it be felt inconvenient, any one may always obviate the inconvenience by keeping a piece of dry bread or a biscuit in his pocket, and taking a piece of it when he finds it needful to do so. This breakfast at the coffee-shop will be a good one, if it consists of a dry toast and a cup of strong coffee; butter, sugar, and milk, are, indeed, very palatable articles, but they are mere luxuries, and, moreover, are not unfrequently positively injurious to those who take them. If, however, something besides the toast and coffee be desirable, then the yolk of an egg may be taken, which being boiled hard and well masticated in eating, will be both palatable and nutritious. The cost of breakfast even with this addition will not be greater than for the very unsuitable meal he will otherwise receive from the ' beer-house.'

There is no time allowed for what in some trades is called ' fours,' but there is commonly an opportunity of getting some porter or ale in the course of the afternoon, and here also caution is needful, for neither of these articles, nor indeed any fermented or spirituous liquor, is very suitable for a tailor, especially when at his work. But as he cannot often procure what would be more suitable, he should take care to drink of these temperately; should he choose malt liquor, and this be at all acid, he may always correct this evil by getting a little of the 'carbonate of soda,' and putting a small quantity of it into the beer; this will neutralize the acid, and the beer, if drank in its state of effervescence, will be much the better for his stomach, while it will be equally palatable as before.

At supper time, the quantity of food taken should always be small, and it should consist of such articles as are most agreeable to the stomach rather than the palate.   Many young men hurt themselves by taking at this meal large quantities of radishes, onions, water-cresses, or other raw vegetables; or it may be that they eat shrimps, crabs, oysters, periwinkles, or such-like fish, that are equally indigestible. To these things they will sometimes add cheese, and their bread will be, as usual, new, or very nearly so.   Upon this hete-rogeneous mass of solid food they will put, perhaps, two or three pints of porter, and probably some spiri-tuous liquor; while, as if to make the mischief as complete as possible, they will smoke a considerable quantity of tobacco, and sit sometimes for several hours in company with a number of men who are similarly employed.   It were a waste of words to de-scribe at length how injurious all this must necessarily be to the health of a young man, perhaps just come from the country, where he has breathed a compara-tively pure air, and has had many other means of pre-serving his health, such as he will not easily find, or even a substitute for them, in a large and crowded city.   The sad consequences of this imprudence are soon perceptible, not only by the subject of it, but also to all around him; and it is well for him when he escapes with no worse consequences than a greatly and constantly disordered stomach, for distressing as this is, it is not the worst, by far, of the effects that may and often do ensue upon such egregious folly as that of which he has been guilty.

But enough has been now said upon this subject to warn such as are disposed to take the warning. To such, however, as are not, it would be only a waste of time to say any thing farther. What has been said must therefore suffice, and this will be found useful if duly regarded.

As to exercise, there certainly are difficulties in the way of taking it regularly and at proper times, but these may to a great extent be obviated by a little prudent management. A good walk, both in the morning and the evening, may be secured by simply taking care to lodge at a considerable distance from the shop, which arrangement will make it necessary to rise in the morning earlier than otherwise it would be, and thus a second benefit will be obtained. There will also probably be the advantage of breathing a somewhat purer atmosphere than that of the crowded city, as a convenient lodging for a single man may be readily found on the skirts of the town, and it is thitherward that his attention should be directed when he seeks for one. If he will but make the experiment he will find himself none the worse, but most likely much the better, both in health and in personal comfort, by having a walk of from two to three miles every day. In addition to this he may often contrive to get a short walk before dinner, and this will prepare him to take that meal with far more advantage than if he sits in the tap-room of an ale-house, and gets to smoking or drinking, as is often done before dinner as well as afterwards. The best way to avoid all temptation to this practice is to refrain altogether from taking his meals at a beer-house, or in any other way making such a place his home.

The next thing that remains to be noticed is, 'respectability of character;' and here it should be understood that a mechanic may be, if he pleases, as respectable as a nobleman in all that goes to make up true respectability. And it is very important that a young man should aim at preserving or attaining this, as hereby he will be sure in the long run to gain the respect of both his master and his fellow-workmen,

and will also, on this account, be likely to secure constant employment, and that too, perhaps, in preference
to a superior workman who is of a disreputable character and appearance.

Masters in general have a decided predilection for
decently-dressed and well-behaved workmen, and seldom fail to show their regard for such, while they will
sometimes discharge a man that is dirty, ragged, and
vulgar, solely on account of these faults.

But highly important as is this respectability, it will
not be likely to be duly valued unless care be taken
to avoid the following evils—for they are really evils,
and great ones too, whatever may be thought or said
to the contrary.

And first, let every young man be careful to have a
bed-room entirely to his own use, as the first step to
his ruin may consist in having a fellow-lodger, especially if he be a dissolute man, and such men as this are
usually very forward in getting an inexperienced youth
to lodge with them, since hereby they can often manage
to indulge their passion for intemperance or for gam-
bling at the expense of another person. No young
man ought therefore to place himself in circumstances
of so much peril. As to the common plea of saving
expense thereby, it is altogether futile, since more than
double, or even treble, the rent of a decent room may
be and often is expended in one night's debauch.

And then let such a one beware of going to the
beer-house in the evening after he leaves work, as he
will thereby be in danger of being 'led on' by con-
firmed sots or by gamblers, until he will fall into their
habits, perhaps almost imperceptibly to himself, and
thus without intending to do any thing more than to
drink a little beer in a social way, and to smoke what
is called a 'friendly pipe,' he will gradually learn to
spend, perhaps, several hours every evening in drinking, smoking, and playing cards, bagatelle, and such-
like games, to the joint injury of his health, his morals,

and his pocket. Besides which, he will be in farther danger of learning to roam the streets late at night, and thus gradually to form associations with dissolute persons, by whose examples and persuasions he will in all probability be led farther onward in folly and vice, and in the end to incurable disease or a premature death.

He should also take care to avoid seeking amusement in company with what are called 'good fellows,' either in the streets, or at fairs, races, theatres, 'free and easy' clubs, odd-fellows' lodges, and the like; as hereby he will doubtless get no good, and the probability is that he will get much harm, by learning habits of idleness and dissipation, for the days as well as the evenings and the nights will be often required for one or other of these amusements.

Moreover, let him be careful how he spends his Sundays, otherwise he will gradually be drawn into the very common, yet very injurious, habit of spending the first half of that day in a listless manner, being neither shaved, washed, nor dressed, and the remainder of it in either tippling at an ale-house, or revelling in a place yet more dangerous to his health and morals.

Let him, on no account, be either unwilling or ashamed to attend the public worship of Almighty God; for there is but little hope of his escaping the manifold temptations that will inevitably beset him if he sets out in life by habitually neglecting the duty he owes to his Maker—and this duty is altogether neglected by perhaps more than ninety out of every hundred men in the trade. He will soon, by the mere habit, overcome all his unwillingness, and he will also soon cease to be annoyed by the jeers of others who, when they see a young man determined to live soberly and rationally, not only soon leave off bantering him, but also ere long will learn to respect him the more for the attention he pays to duties which, with all their seeming contempt of them, they are still conscious are incumbent upon themselves.

There will be plenty of time in the intervals between the morning and the evening services for either reading,* walking, or any other becoming recreation, and in fine weather a pleasant and healthful evening walk may be secured by attending public worship in one or other of the adjacent villages; and in this case he will find himself far better prepared for his to-morrow's work than he would have been had he spent the same time at an ale-house, or even at a tea-garden.

If he attends to these admonitions and counsels, he will ultimately find that, although he may not be able to command great wealth, or fame, or station, he will both acquire and enjoy what is far better than all these together, namely, good health, a peaceful and contented mind, a fair reputation, and in general as much money as will enable him to procure all the necessaries and many of the comforts of life. And should he at any subsequent time be enabled to become a master, he will be all the more likely to succeed well in that capacity, for having been an industrious, careful, and well-behaved journeyman. Such cases are by no means rare, and although all cannot be masters, much less wealthy masters, yet all may be worthy and intelligent men, and, being such, may reasonably look for a sufficient maintenance, and also for much real and lasting enjoyment.

* There will be no difficulty in finding time to read on other days as well as on Sundays, if there be a desire to do so. And there will be such a desire wherever there is any perception of the value of this exercise as a means of useful instruction, combined with endlessly diversified amusement. There are now ample opportunities for reading at all the more respectable of the coffee-shops, where, for a much less sum than is usually spent at the beer-house, a comfortable supper may be had, together with the opportunity of quietly perusing many valuable publications.

THE END.

A. SWEETING, PRINTER, BARTLETT'S BUILDINGS, HOLBORN.

e·due date.

——————————

——————————

——————————

——————————

——————————

——————————

——————————

——————————

——————————

——————————

——————————

——————————

A, BERKELEY
20
℗s

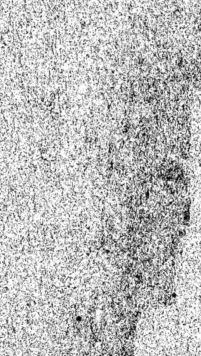

CPSIA information can be obtained
at www.ICGtesting.com
Printed in the USA
BVHW040914211218
536170BV00015B/430/P